THE VOICE OF THE
UNDERDOG

◇◇◇◇◇◇

Paperback Publication Date: 2020

E-Book Publication Date: 2020

ISBN: 978-1-7347799-0-5 (paperback)

ISBN: 978-1-7347799-1-2 (electronic)

First Edition Published 2020

BizComPress

A division of BizCom Associates

BizComPress.com

1400 Preston Rd. #305, Plano, TX 75093

Printed in the United States of America

THE VOICE OF THE
UNDERDOG®

HOW CHALLENGER BRANDS
CREATE DISTINCTION BY THINKING
CULTURE FIRST

MIKE SULLIVAN & MICHAEL TUGGLE

For Melinda, Regan and Jack

For Ginger, Matt and Caroline

This is all for you.

CONTENTS

PREFACE

∞∞∞∞

There's an awful lot written on the subject of branding, but far less about a special group of brands called "challengers." By strict definition, any brand that isn't a category leader is a challenger, but that's not very satisfying or inspiring, and certainly not special. At least not by definition alone.

In this book, my co-author and I will describe the true essence of challenger brands along with ideas about how successful challengers of all sizes use culture to create extraordinary brand distinction. We think a lot about brands and company culture at The LOOMIS Agency, but this isn't a book about our agency, and it's not filled with case studies about our clients, although we've included a few here and there. In fact, we'll kick things off with one such story in the Introduction that follows.

This is a book about what we believe is a poorly understood and grossly underleveraged connection between brand and culture. We offer our observations and clarify them with examples and stories in service to underdogs of all varieties across all categories be they

B2C, B2B, or both. The subject is especially relevant for leaders running companies where ambitions run high but resources are modest. What my co-author and I address in the chapters that follow is the way leaders can cultivate unassailable competitive advantages by simply bringing more intention to the way their brands align with their cultures and vice versa.

About ten years ago, we decided LOOMIS would go all in on the cause, and we committed our agency to an exclusive focus on challenger brands. Today, we're the country's leading challenger brand advertising agency. While I count many faithful comrades in our fight for the underdog, none has met my enthusiasm with more gusto than my co-author, Michael Tuggle. It was at Michael's unyielding encouragement that I finally agreed to produce this long overdue work, and it certainly would not have happened without him.

In the pages ahead, we trace the many thoughts and ideas produced by countless hours of discussion and work and hundreds of blog posts on a topic that should be on the mind of any leader who believes that outthinking the competition is better than outspending them.

— Mike Sullivan

INTRODUCTION

◇◇◇◇◇◇

BRANDS WITH THE BEST CULTURE WIN

Back in 2009, I participated in a challenger branding workshop held at the Silicon Valley headquarters of YAHOO! that would fundamentally change the way I thought about what our advertising agency was all about. At the time, nobody was talking much about challenger brands. But over the course of the two-day experience, it became crystal clear to me that thinking and behaving like a challenger brand wasn't just *relevant* to every entrepreneurially minded CEO at the workshop. It was transformative. At least to me.

The credit for that shift in mindset goes entirely to the London-based challenger brand consultancy, Eat Big Fish, and in particular to EBF partner Mark Barden, who conducted that particular workshop. As an advertising professional, I'd previously thought of challenger brands as brands defined simply by a specific kind of advertising claim based on their subordinated marketplace position. As marketing students, we all learned about the challenger position taken up by Avis when the company famously turned its secondary status to advantage, claiming "Avis is only number two in rental cars, so we try harder." Of course, the Pepsi Challenge took the idea one step further inviting consumers to taste the difference for themselves, which I happily did in grocery stores as a kid. Indeed, I did find the sweeter taste of Pepsi more appealing than Coke and, thanks to a little bit of cola sampling genius, our household flipped to the second-placed brand.

But the ideas that drive the concept of challenger branding are much bigger and more potent than clever ad campaigns rooted in a twist or turn on runners-up claims. Challenger branding is masterfully described in EBF founder Adam Morgan's seminal book on the topic, aptly titled, *Eating the Big Fish: How Challenger Brands Can Compete Against Brand Leaders*. Challenger brands can't spend their way to success with big ad campaigns like category leaders. Instead, they start with business strategy and identify opportunities for disruption that make the marketer's job far easier than it would be otherwise. That's because challenger strategies are born of unique differences fueled by an organic power that attracts an audience.

True challengers don't follow convention. Instead, they expose the weakness of category norms with alternatives that often appear obvious with the perfect vision of hindsight. Challengers zig while others zag, and generally wreak havoc on competitors by showing up in a way that's anything but expected. Challengers take consumers and competitors alike by surprise, which in turn provokes something every marketer desperately wants and needs—*a response*. Love them or hate them, challengers will not be ignored.

At the challenger workshop in Silicon Valley, I happened to

meet the founder and CEO of a regional retail chain of mattress stores who was puzzling over a problem many marketers face. He wanted to know how he could create real brand distinction and drive more retail traffic in his highly commoditized category. The Great Recession was just beginning to gain its head of steam and consumer wallets were tightening fast. Little did we know how bad things were going to get.

A few months after meeting at the workshop, I got a call from the CEO asking if we'd like to handle his advertising account. His mattress chain was still struggling with traffic, and sales had gone from slow to sluggish across his thirty locations. By now the economy was in full seizure. Retailers across all categories were shifting into survival mode and the CEO was very near panic. With sales trending fast in the wrong direction, the idea of differentiating his brand and driving store traffic had escalated from important to urgent. He needed an idea to turn up the volume, and he needed it quickly.

The concepts Mark Barden shared at the challenger workshop were fresh on my mind as our ad agency tackled the CEO's problem. It's tempting to focus on advertising messaging and media levels when sales are weak, but we knew this wasn't simply an advertising problem. Besides, the CEO had no more money to spend on media, and his messaging was on par with the rest of the category. Mattresses are always on sale, after all.

We knew the brand had to do something to disrupt the market, and it needed to be rooted in a point of difference. But not just any difference. It had to be a difference that customers would find important and engaging, especially given the context of a faltering economy and stingy spending on discretionary products like mattresses. As part of our research, we sent agency team members on field trips posing as mattress shoppers. They shopped our client, and they shopped his competitors, and they came back with an insight. The answer to our new client's dilemma lay hidden in operations and his company's extraordinary commitment to sales process and training.

The mattress CEO was relentless about doing right by customers, and this made him very particular about hiring and training. The company's extensive sales training far exceeded that of competitors, and the result was a genuinely superior customer experience. His salespeople behaved more like knowledgeable consultants than the typical high-pressured hucksters who give the retail mattress category its well-deserved bad rap. And, as we did our research, we happened upon a critically important detail that would turn out to be this client's challenger brand rocket fuel.

Because the chain's sales practices were famously low-pressure and informative in nature, customers routinely purchased the right mattress for their needs. The CEO surmised that his company's superior approach to sales was the reason their average ticket exceeded the industry's. He never gave much thought, however, to the company's far below average product return rate, which was also a byproduct of sales methods that prioritized customer satisfaction over a fast buck.

In fact, the number of returns for our client's mattress chain were inconsequential compared to the balance of the category and especially low by comparison with the category leader, a brand well known for their hard-closing conquest approach to sales. This was a significant but hidden challenger advantage, and our client hadn't leveraged it at all. On the contrary, his chain had been following the category norm for mattress returns, which was a particular pain point for customers. The category's standard 30-day return policies are intentionally and notoriously draconian because, as anyone who has ever shopped for a mattress knows, high-pressure mattress sales practices result in extreme levels of post-purchase dissatisfaction. Making it easy for customers to return the product would devastate operations and sales for most chains in the mattress category.

The way the category was zigging in this respect presented the perfect opportunity for our new client to zag. So, our agency made a bold recommendation straight out of the challenger branding playbook. We told the CEO to overhaul his return policy and make it not only easier for customers to return products they were unhappy with, but to give them one full year to sleep on their decision.

A month later, we rolled out an advertising campaign promoting the mattress category's first and only no-questions-asked, one-year money-back guarantee. It was a revolutionary challenger move that turned category convention on its ear and, in so doing, caused sales to spike thirty percent the very first month. That quick success was followed by months on end of year-over-year double-digit increases that climbed as high as fifty percent. Our favorite part of this challenger success story was an attempt by category killer Mattress Firm to match our client's one-year offer only to yank it back quickly after being swamped with returns. Mattress Firm hadn't operationalized the consultative sales approach like our client had, so the poor result for them was inevitable.

This fact underscores an important lesson the folks at Eat Big Fish take great pains to drive home: challengers have to be willing and able to do something competitors can't or simply won't do in order to create clear and relevant distinction for their brand. The magic wasn't in our client's one-year guarantee. It was in the many hours of training each of the company's sales associates had to go through before hitting their showroom floors. It was this long-standing focus on selling the right way that made such an audacious guarantee possible at all. Our client had operationalized a sales process that wasn't easy to detect by competitors and no easier to replicate by any who had.

Intentional or otherwise, the CEO's focus on sales had created a true brand advantage for his company, and that advantage made the job of advertising easy. Even the best advertising is no substitute for meaningful brand distinction anchored to a real consumer insight. Challengers that understand this and are willing to do what it takes to create a genuine distinction are awfully hard to beat.

But there was a second important lesson buried in our client's success that has become even more evident to me in the years since we hit that first challenger home run. Our mattress client's sales process was supported and reinforced by something far more powerful than top-down mandates and training alone. The company's focus on customer service was an endemic part of the company's culture from stem to stern. You might even say it was the basis of the company's culture. As such, it functioned as a reliable guide for the behavior and performance of all the company's employees, not just the salespeople. From all sides, the company's culture served as a virtual feedback loop that held everyone to a higher standard of customer care, which turned out to be uncommon for the mattress category. It was this commitment that created the opportunity to offer customers a significant benefit that no competitor could match. Another more obvious lesson that might be drawn is that great service pays. But the much bigger lesson is that for companies counting on the performance of people, culture is inextricably linked to brand performance in ways that aren't always obvious at first glance.

This is the central idea explored in this book. Company culture serves as the most fundamental challenger brand advantage there is. When companies get their cultures and their brands working in synchronicity, powerful things begin to take shape and only some of those things have anything to do with advertising and marketing, at least explicitly.

From recruiting the right talent to attracting more customers, the harmony created when a company's culture and brand are in sync can produce the kind of magnetic draw that makes a challenger brand tough to beat. What we explore in the chapters that follow is how leaders can cultivate durable competitive advantages by simply bringing more intention to the way their brands align with their cultures and vice versa.

Brands with the best cultures are most often the ones that win.

1

OUR LOVE AFFAIR
WITH THE UNDERDOG

We love the underdog.

It's not a fleeting love. It's not a flirtatious love we can take or leave. It's not a love we ever really outgrow. As human beings, our love for the underdog and our desire to cheer for the challenger against overwhelming odds isn't simply a learned social convention or the pull to join the crowd. It's a primal evolutionary trigger. A mix of sympathy, empathy, competition, a sense of fairness, and in some cases, a healthy dash of schadenfreude thrown in for good measure.

Why do we care so much about underdogs and challengers? On the surface, it could stem from our innate intolerance of bullies, the notion that it's unfair to pick on someone or something smaller than yourself, coupled with our competitive nature. But if you dig a little deeper, there are four other integral reasons we love to cheer for the underdog.

One, we love a great story. From early cave dwellers to the ancient Greeks, and from Shakespeare to modern authors, every civilization the world has ever known has had and revered people who could tell a great story, and we are no different. Stories help us see our place in the world. They frame light and dark, right and wrong, life and death. Underdog stories give us something to cheer for and, often, something to aspire to. There are no stories more heartwarming or more inspirational than those of challengers overcoming unbeatable odds.

Two, underdogs are universal. Every culture has "haves" and "have nots." Those who are blessed and those who are less fortunate. And whether an underdog is defined by their physical size, race, gender, nationality, orientation, political views, or religious affiliation, we can all recognize them. We know how the underdog's story ends most of the time. But we've also seen them pull the upset. To win against every conceivable odd. That's what we cheer for.

Three, when we look at challengers, we see ourselves. No matter how our personal stories have unfolded, at one time or another, we've all found ourselves in the role of the underdog. On any given day, any one of us could be the underdog. Fighting against the odds. Battling the unfair. Because of that, it's easier for us to empathize with others fighting uphill battles.

Four, underdogs prove anything is possible. Just as the night is always darkest before the dawn, the moment when the odds seem the most impossible are often when those with bigger hearts remind us that miracles can happen. On an ice rink in Lake Placid. In a boxing ring in Tokyo. On a basketball court in March. Underdogs give us hope. Not just for their futures, but for our own.

Our love of the challenger extends across every facet of our lives from sports and entertainment, to business and philanthropy, to religion and politics. Take a good look around and you'll find underdogs are just about everywhere.

∞∞∞∞

SPORTS

Because they are rooted in head-to-head competition, our most notable underdog stories come from the world of sports. The word itself originated in the 19th century to describe the losing animal in a dog fight because he was literally "under" the winning dog.

Since then, in almost every athletic contest, there has been a favorite and an underdog because of their records, their history, their talent, or simply because the betting line predicts which team or athlete will win and by how much. And while there is always some expectation as to who will win, at least in professional sports, the vast majority of these contests are played out without any real drama or any real surprise.

In the NFL, NBA, NHL, MLB and MLS, are we really shocked when any one team beats another? Take Major League Baseball. Since the League moved to the 162-game season in 1961, only two teams—the 1998 New York Yankees and the 2001 Seattle Mariners—have finished the season with a winning percentage over .700. That means in over fifty-seven seasons and more than 138,000 baseball games, even the best teams were beaten three times out of ten.

In an era of salary caps, free agency, and superior training, most sporting events turn out as expected. But every now and then, a story bubbles up that is so unexpected, so inspiring, and so spectacular in its drama that it becomes part of the enduring underdog mythology. A story that is somehow bigger than itself where we find ourselves cheering for a team or an individual we didn't even know in a moment that echoes forever. How many of these do you remember?

◇◇◇◇◇◇◇

THE GUARANTEE

Three days before Super Bowl III, underdog Jets quarterback Joe Namath guarantees a win against the heavily favored Baltimore Colts. During the season, Baltimore had posted a 13-1 record and had blown out the Browns in the NFL Championship game 34-0, while the Jets had squeaked by the Oakland Raiders 27-23 in the AFL Championship. The Colts defense led the league in fewest points allowed, and their offense ranked second in the league for points scored. Few thought the Jets had a chance, but on Super Sunday, Namath delivered a 16-7 victory that is still considered one of the greatest upsets of all time.

◇◇◇◇◇◇◇

THE LANDING

In 1976, the Japanese Men's Gymnastics team came to the Montreal Olympics looking to win their fifth team gold medal in a row. But standing in their way was an extremely talented team from the Soviet Union, equally determined to end the Japanese dynasty. In the finals of the team competition, one of Japan's best gymnasts, Shun Fujimoto, severely injured his knee on his first rotation: the floor exercise. But he told no one.

On his next rotation, the pommel horse, Shun fought through the pain and put up a solid score. But then came his third rotation, the rings. It was Shun's best event and despite his injured knee, he performed a nearly flawless routine. All he had left was his dismount. Flying through the air in excruciating pain, Shun stuck his landing from ten feet up, dislocating his knee and tearing his ligaments. Unable to continue, Shun was forced to withdraw from the final three rotations but his 9.7 score on rings ultimately helped secure the team gold for Japan.

∞∞∞∞∞∞

MIRACLE ON ICE

The U.S. Men's hockey team beating the Russians at the 1980 Lake Placid Olympics is considered by many to be the greatest upset in sports history, made forever immortal by Al Michaels' iconic call, "Do you believe in miracles?" The Russians had dominated the U.S. for decades but as Herb Brooks reminded his team before taking the ice, "If we played them ten times, they might win nine. But not tonight." The U.S. beat the Soviets in the first game of the medal round 3-2 and then secured the gold medal beating Finland 4-2 in their final game.

COOL RUNNINGS

At the 1988 Calgary Olympics, the Caribbean island nation of Jamaica competed in the Four-Man Bobsled for the first time in history. They weren't fast, and they didn't win a medal. Didn't even come close. But the nation where snow and ice are simply a concept captured everyone's attention and modeled for the world the very spirit of the Olympic Creed—"The most important thing in the Olympic Games is not to win but to take part, just as the most important thing in life is not the triumph but the struggle. The essential thing is not to have conquered but to have fought well."

EDDIE THE EAGLE

Also at the 1988 Calgary Olympics, while the Jamaicans were feeling the love at the bobsled run, an unexpected eagle was soaring over at the ski jump. Sort of. That year, among the highfliers from Finland, Norway, Czechoslovakia, and Yugoslavia, there was an Englishman in Coke-bottle glasses named Eddie Edwards who became the first man in sixty years to represent Great Britain in the ski jump. Part in jest, but part in love, people started calling Edwards "Eddie the Eagle." And while he finished next to last in the standings, his heart-warming story and determination made him one of Calgary's biggest stars.

THE KNOCKOUT

When Buster Douglas stepped into the ring with Heavyweight Champion Mike Tyson on February 11, 1990, the question wasn't whether he could win. It was how fast Tyson would knock him out. Tyson was undefeated, having never been knocked down, and Douglas was a 42-1 underdog with a mixed past and a so-so record. His mother had just passed away, the bout was in Tokyo, and nobody expected it to last long. But it did. Douglas took the best Tyson had and despite being knocked down in the eighth round, Douglas stunned the world by knocking Tyson out in the tenth. To this day, many consider it the greatest upset in boxing history.

YOU CAN DO IT!

At the 1996 Olympics in Atlanta, the U.S. Women's Gymnastics team was making an improbable run at the team gold medal. They were locked in a fierce battle with the Russians and the Romanians and, in the end, everything came down to Kerri Strug on the vault. On her first attempt, Strug underrotated the landing and severely injured her ankle. With the gold medal still in the balance, and her coach Béla Károlyi chanting, "You can do it, Kerri," Strug bravely stepped up, sprinted down the runway, and landed her second vault on one foot before collapsing in pain. She scored a 9.712, securing the gold for "The Magnificent Seven" and forever cementing her place in Olympic history.

⋄⋄⋄⋄⋄⋄⋄

DETHRONING THE BEAR

Russian Greco-Roman wrestler Aleksandr Karelin is arguably the most dominant athlete there has ever been, posting an obscene lifetime record of 887 wins and just two losses. Nicknamed "The Russian Bear," "Alexander The Great," and "The Experiment," three-time gold medalist Karelin was riding a thirteen-year winning streak coming into the 2000 Olympics in Sydney and had not surrendered a point in competition in more than six years. By comparison, his finals opponent, American wrestler Rulon Gardner, had exceeded all expectations just by making it to the gold medal match. But that wasn't enough for him. Using a strong defense that kept Karelin off balance, Gardner pushed the match to overtime and pulled off one of the greatest Olympic miracles ever, beating Karelin 1-0 to take the gold medal.

⋄⋄⋄⋄⋄⋄⋄

HOT AS A PISTOL

February 15, 2006, was like most game days at Greece Athena High School in Rochester, New York. The basketball team was playing hard, and student manager Jason McElwain was sitting on the bench cheering them on. Jason had a high-functioning form of autism, and while he'd never played in a game, he worked every bit as hard as the kids on the floor.

That night, to reward Jason for his hard work as manager, the coach let Jason wear an actual jersey and sit on the bench next to the team. But then with 4:19 left in the second half, the coach decided to let Jason play. The stands erupted, and the student cheering section went crazy. He immediately threw up two bricks that weren't even close. But then, according to Jason, he "got hot as a pistol." He launched a three-pointer from the corner that hit nothing but net. Then another one. And another one. And another three after that. In all, Jason scored twenty points hitting a long three at the buzzer before being swarmed by his fans and carried off the court on the shoulders on his teammates. The videos of his performance have been viewed millions of times on YouTube and his performance earned Jason the ESPY Award for the "Best Moment" in 2006.

◇◇◇◇◇◇

UPSET AT THE BIG HOUSE

At the beginning of every college football season, big schools like to ease into their schedule with teams that aren't any kind of threat. Often, they play smaller schools that are just thrilled to play in a big venue where they get half the gate. In 2007, Michigan opened the season at number five in the polls and figured Appalachian State would be a nice way to ease into their season. Nobody told

Appy State the game was supposed to be a layup. For four quarters, Appalachian State hung around and hung around, trading leads with Michigan until finally, with six seconds left, Michigan lined up for a chip shot field goal to win. Appalachian State blocked it and secured one of the greatest upsets in the history of college football.

◇◇◇◇◇◇

CINDERELLA TAKES DOWN NUMBER ONE

From the time the NCAA Division I Men's Basketball tournament went to a sixty-four-team bracket in 1985, the question in every opening round was, "Could a sixteen-seed beat a one-seed?" The answer, of course, was no. Every March, announcers worked hard to make the sixteen-versus-one matchups sound competitive and over the years, there were a few close calls. But for thirty-two years, Cinderella was nowhere to be seen in round one of March Madness. But everyone knew she wouldn't wait forever.

In 2018, sixteen-seed UMBC found themselves matched up with UVA, the top overall seed in the tournament. That meant of the sixty-four teams in the bracket, the University of Maryland-Baltimore County was sixty-fourth and Virginia was first. The teams literally couldn't have been farther apart, and the game was a blowout. But it was not what anyone outside the Retrievers' locker room had expected. From the opening tip, UMBC took it to UVA, and by the middle of the second half, the game was over. There was no buzzer beater. No miracle from half court. UMBC drummed Virginia 74-54 and even though they lost a heartbreaker to Kansas

State in the Round of 32, they will forever be remembered as the first sixteen-seed to ever take down a one-seed in the NCAA Men's Tournament.

◇◇◇◇◇◇

TIGER ROARS AGAIN

In golf, every generation has had a player who transcends the game. Bobby Jones. Ben Hogan. Arnold Palmer. Jack Nicklaus. And then there's Tiger. A golf prodigy from the age of two, Tiger Woods exploded onto the golf scene at sixteen winning three straight U.S. Junior Amateur titles followed by three U.S. Amateur titles and the NCAA National Championship. When Tiger turned pro at twenty in 1996, he ignited both the PGA and the golf world like a house on fire. From 1996 to 2013, Tiger won seventy-nine tournaments including fourteen majors. He made north of $769 million in prize money and endorsements, and he personally elevated the game of golf so dramatically that developers started building golf courses coast to coast to keep up with the demand of people picking up the game for the first time.

The following years, however, saw the house of Tiger start to crumble. In 2010, his marriage to Elin Nordegren ended thanks to numerous alleged affairs. Injuries led to multiple back surgeries accompanied by an addiction to painkillers, a DUI arrest and rehab. Inconceivably, Tiger dropped out of the Top 1,000 rankings. He was done. But he was also Tiger.

In 2017, he slowly started putting his game back together and, by 2018, he showed signs of being competitive. Tiger shocked everyone by winning the 2018 PGA Tour Championship, but most wrote it off to a single great week. It was just one tournament. The following April, when Tiger stepped up to the first tee at Augusta National, he wasn't anyone's favorite to win the 2019 Masters. Sure, he'd won it four times before, but the current field was too talented, and Tiger wasn't the Tiger of old. That's what made his Sunday come from behind charge on the back nine to win his fifth green jacket and his fifteenth major all the more incredible. Sportscasters and news outlets called Tiger winning another major the greatest comeback in sports history. They might just be right.

◇◇◇◇◇◇

ENTERTAINMENT

Within the context of sports, it's easy to understand our fascination with the underdog and why it moves us the way it does. It's fun. It's exciting. And, collectively, it allows us, at least peripherally, to take the hero's journey. To try to overcome incredible odds to triumph in the end. But it's not just in sports that we see it. It's everywhere.

Look at the films that have won the Academy Award for Best Picture in the last thirty-two years. Of the winners, twenty-three have focused on underdog narratives.

Parasite (2020)—A destitute South Korean family schemes their way into the employment of a rich family, setting in motion devastating consequences that destroy three families. (*Parasite* is the first non-English speaking film to win Best Picture placing it among the greatest underdog victories in Oscar history.)

Green Book (2019)—A white, barely literate bouncer from New York agrees to drive and protect an erudite African-American pianist on a concert tour through the deep South in 1962.

The Shape Of Water (2018)—A mute woman working in a top-secret government facility falls in love with an Amazonian fishman whom she saves from execution.

Moonlight (2017)—An African-American man raised by a drug-addicted mother wrestles with his burgeoning homosexuality.

Spotlight (2016)—An investigative team at The Boston Globe fights the Catholic Church to expose a widespread sexual abuse scandal.

12 Years A Slave (2014)—In the pre-Civil War era, free black man Solomon Northrup is kidnapped and sold into slavery where he spends twelve years fighting his way back to his family.

Argo (2013)—A small CIA team uses the ruse of shooting a science fiction film to rescue six U.S. diplomats being held in Tehran during the Iran hostage crisis.

The King's Speech (2011)—England's King George VI fights to learn how to speak without a debilitating stammer before assuming the crown.

The Hurt Locker (2010)—A small band of Army explosives disposal experts try to protect American troops and survive in the midst of the Iraq war.

Slumdog Millionaire (2009)—A kid from the slums of Mumbai uses an appearance on the Indian version of "Who Wants To Be A Millionaire" to set his life straight.

Million Dollar Baby (2005)—A female boxer wins over a crusty old trainer who ultimately becomes her savior inside the ring and out.

Lord of the Rings: Return Of The King (2004)—A lowly hobbit completes an impossible journey to return a magic ring back to the fires of Mount Doom.

A Beautiful Mind (2002)—Brilliant mathematician John Nash fights through schizophrenia to become a Princeton professor, ultimately winning the Nobel Prize.

Gladiator (2001)—A Roman general is betrayed and sold into slavery, ultimately taking revenge as Rome's greatest gladiator.

Shakespeare in Love (1999)—A woman in Elizabethan England

has an affair with Shakespeare and dresses as a man to perform in his plays. (Shakespeare in Love winning Best Picture over Saving Private Ryan is also considered one of the greatest upsets in Oscar history.)

Titanic (1998)—A poor street rat befriends a high society girl on the world's grandest ocean liner before tragedy tears them apart.

Braveheart (1996)—William Wallace uses the murder of his wife to fuel a rebellion that ultimately leads Scotland to independence.

Forrest Gump (1995)—A slow-witted, kind-hearted man witnesses decades of significant twentieth-century events, saving soul after soul in the process.

Schindler's List (1994)—Oskar Schindler, a member of the Nazi party, saves more than a thousand Jews from the Holocaust by employing them in his factory.

Silence of the Lambs (1992)—A young FBI trainee fights inexperience and sexism to get inside the head of one serial killer to try to catch another.

Dances With Wolves (1991)—An American soldier, alone on a frontier outpost, brokers peace with area Native Americans by understanding and becoming one of them.

Driving Miss Daisy (1990)—An African-American chauffeur and an old Jewish woman from Atlanta develop an unlikely friendship.

Rain Man (1989)—On a cross country journey, a young hustler tries to reconnect emotionally with the autistic savant brother he never knew he had.

And those are just the Best Picture winners. From *Rocky* to *Rudy*, from *Hoosiers* to *The Bad News Bears*, and from *Remember The Titans* to *Friday Night Lights*, there are dozens of wonderful, heartwarming, and inspiring movies about underdogs that aren't just good. They are beloved.

The same goes for the plays and musicals we love on the stage. Right now on Broadway, audiences are cheering musicals like *Hamilton* (a Caribbean orphan finds his way to New York, then fights to become George Washington's right-hand man and one of the Founding Fathers), *Dear Evan Hansen* (a socially awkward teenager gets wrapped up in a sweeping lie trying to find his place in the world), *Mean Girls* (a new teenage girl tries to find her place among a brutal collection of high school cliques including "the plastics"), *Wicked* (the real story behind Oz's Wicked Witch of the West), *The Phantom Of The Opera* (a disfigured man haunts the Paris Opera House to be close to the woman he loves), *Waitress* (a pregnant waitress in an abusive relationship turns to baking and her doctor to find a way out), and *The Book of Mormon* (two young Mormon elders are sent on a mission to help convert Africans to Christianity, facing off with a Ugandan warlord in the process). Whether dramatic or comedic, at their hearts, they are all underdog stories.

Not surprisingly, television reflects the same trends as film and stage, although in a strikingly different format. While dramas and comedies have been television staples since the 1950s, the biggest trend in TV programming over the past twenty-five years has undisputedly been the rise of "reality TV." From competitive shows like *Survivor, America's Got Talent, The Voice, The Amazing Race, American Idol,* and *The Biggest Loser* to documentary-style shows like *I Am Jazz* (the journey of a transgender teen), *Born This Way* (a group of friends with Down Syndrome come of age searching for their independence), and *Extreme Makeover: Home Edition* (inspiring families who need a break are given a whole new home built in a week), our fascination with underdogs has been fed like never before with dozens of shows we can literally watch every night. While it's true the "reality TV" movement was started because reality series were cheaper to shoot than comedies and dramas, the truth remains that if viewers didn't connect with them, they never would have lasted.

<><><><><><>

RELIGION AND POLITICS

It's no great shock that the creative world of entertainment is largely built on stories about challengers and overcoming the odds. But what may be surprising is when we shift that lens to the world at large we find just as many challenger stories, and we seem to be just as captivated by them.

Look at the origin stories for Christianity and Judaism,

America's two largest religions. Jesus didn't suddenly emerge as some great military leader. He was born in a stable to a teenage mother and worked as a lowly carpenter. His three-year ministry was the very definition of an underdog challenging the status quo and, ultimately, it was that fight against the establishment that got him crucified. Like Jesus, Moses had an extremely humble beginning being born under an edict from Pharaoh to kill every male Hebrew child. Moses was only saved by the bravery of his mother who hid him among the bulrushes at the edge of the Nile in the hope he would be found and adopted. As we know from Exodus, Moses was saved by Pharaoh's daughter, grew up side-by-side with Ramses, and ultimately rejected his privilege and his adoptive brother to lead his people out of slavery. Noah built the ark when everyone thought he was crazy. Joseph was sold into slavery by his brothers before ultimately serving Pharaoh and saving all of Egypt. And we all know the greatest underdog tale ever—the story of David and Goliath.

In today's vernacular, any time we talk about an outmatched challenger taking on insurmountable odds, that's what we call it: David versus Goliath. The boy taking on a man. The smaller and outmatched taking on the stronger and seemingly more capable. The outsider taking on the established champion. Over two and a half centuries of American politics, the David and Goliath narrative has popped up countless times in races at every level. But it's worth considering whether it has ever dominated the landscape like it has during the past twelve years.

In 2008, Hillary Clinton was primed to run against John McCain for President. That, in and of itself, was set to be a great underdog story as no woman had ever represented her party as the nominee for President. Running against a strong, albeit expected Republican challenger who was older, white, and a Senate fixture, would set up an unprecedented underdog story. It turned out, the Democrats had another underdog narrative in mind, nominating a young, dynamic, African-American first-term Senator named Barack Obama on a platform of "Hope and Change." At the Republican National Convention, the Republicans pulled a challenger rabbit out of their own hat, nominating virtual unknown, Alaska Governor Sarah Palin to serve as John McCain's Vice President, but it wasn't enough to derail the Obama Express.

As unlikely as President Obama's election had seemed in 2008, no one could have foreseen the underdog narrative that played out in the 2016 election for President. On June 16, 2015, when Donald Trump descended the escalator in Trump Tower and announced he was running for President of the United States, *everyone* thought it was a publicity stunt. Trump had talked about running for President in 1988, but he didn't. Then he briefly ran as a Reform Party candidate in 2000. He talked about it in 2004 and again before 2012. But the talk never turned into a serious campaign. 2016 looked like another publicity grab for a man constantly in the spotlight. An outsider willing to say and do just about anything without the least fear of repercussions. But this time, something unexpected happened.

As the months rolled on, Trump's say-anything, nationalistic bravado started landing and sticking with Conservatives around the country and, more importantly, with an entire constituency in the "flyover states" that the Democratic Party, the press, and the pollsters seemed not to know even existed. In large part, these voters in the center of the country viewed themselves as voiceless underdogs who had quietly watched from the heartland while the coasts and the big cities played kingmaker election after election. But this was different. Donald Trump was talking to them. He acknowledged them. He visited them time and time and time again, and by the summer of 2016, he was speaking not just to them, but for them. And on November 8, 2016, backed by voters who, to many, seemingly came out of nowhere, Donald Trump pulled off one of the greatest upsets in American politics and became the forty-fifth President of the United States.

In the last twenty years, starting with President Clinton's impeachment and moving through the tenures of Presidents Bush, Obama, and now Trump, our country has become more divided politically than ever before. Progress within the parties seems to have ground to a halt, while compromise and reaching across the aisle seems downright anachronistic. Americans seem to be further apart on the issues than we've ever been, and we now find ourselves more than $21 trillion in debt. With that as a backdrop, the rallying cry for new candidates has been that Washington needs new leaders willing to govern in a way that breaks with the Liberal and Conservative conventions of the past. Voters have been looking for outsiders who will bring to Washington a new way of governing that will break the toxic gridlock that divides us.

In the 2018 cycle, that movement was embodied by campaigns from firebrand candidates like Alexandria Ocasio-Cortez in New York and Beto O'Rourke in Texas. While O'Rourke lost in the General, Ocasio-Cortez headlined a wave of historic victories that included her becoming the youngest woman ever elected to Congress at twenty-nine, Rashida Tlaib and Ilhan Omar becoming the first Muslim women elected to Congress, and Sharice Davids and Debra Haaland becoming the first Native American women ever elected to Congress. In Vermont, a transgender woman named Christine Hallquist won the Democratic Gubernatorial primary falling short in the General, but in Colorado, Jared Polis was elected as the first openly gay male Governor in the country. And in both parties, more and more underdogs are running and winning. More women. More minorities. More business leaders. More veterans. More LGBTQ candidates. More "outsiders." Across the country, we're not just cheering for the underdogs. We're electing them.

∞∞∞∞

SOCIETY

People are also reaching out to help fellow challengers in unprecedented ways. According to the Kickstarter website, since the crowdfunding site was founded in April, 2009, more than sixteen million people have contributed more than $4 billion to support more than 157,000 creative projects. At the same time, more than fifty million donors have contributed more than $5 billion to GoFundMe fundraisers helping those less fortunate and people in need.

Much is made of all the ways the United States comes up short. But according to Giving USA, a public service initiative of The Giving Institute, Americans contributed more than $400 billion to charity in 2017. To put that in perspective, $400 billion is more than the individual GDPs of South Africa, Ireland, Israel, Hong Kong, Denmark, Singapore, Finland, the Czech Republic, or New Zealand in the same year. We don't just love the underdogs in our country. We embrace them. Are there opportunities to do more? Of course. But no country on the planet offers challengers a better opportunity to compete and win than the United States.

We do it for them. But we also do it for ourselves. For most of us, it's part of who we are. For all of our dysfunction, we are a country of opportunity and a country of optimism forever believing that tomorrow will be better than today. That's why every night, at the end of our national newscasts, the networks don't end with crime. They don't end with war. They don't end with misfortune. Instead, you'll hear something like this:

> *And finally tonight, the story of a Good Samaritan—a first responder who crawled across a frozen pond to rescue a dog that had fallen in. A two year old who was lost in the woods for three days was found today. A startup company is succeeding against all odds. A homeless man who found a bank bag with $20,000 returned it to the owner today. A nurse who spent her holidays with her patients so they wouldn't be alone. A young Leukemia patient got to ride in a fire truck. The parents of a young woman killed by a drunk driver got a visit from the young man who received their daughter's heart, and listened again to her heart, this time, beating inside his chest.*

We are a nation of challengers with underdog stories all around us. We can't escape them. But then again, why would we want to?

2

⟡⟡⟡⟡⟡⟡

WHAT CHALLENGER BRANDS
ARE AND ARE NOT

As it turns out, the prom queen lives in a trailer park.

At the 2007 California State Fair Wine Competition, the Charles Shaw Chardonnay, affectionately known to Californians as "Two Buck Chuck" because of its $1.99 price tag, took the top prize beating out 350 other Chardonnays from all over California. Second place went to a lovely $18 bottle of wine from Napa Valley, while the most expensive Chardonnays in the competition—bottles that topped out around $55—didn't even place.

It was a feather in the cap of one of America's most cost-conscious winemakers, but not the first and certainly not a fluke. Even before the 2005 Chardonnay was named "Best of California" and "Best of Show" at the 2007 Fair with a score of 98 and a double gold medal, the Charles Shaw Shiraz bested twenty-three hundred other wines at the 2002 International Eastern Wine Competition. That win was nice. But winning in California? That shook the foundation.

The wine competition at the California State Fair is billed as "the oldest, most prestigious wine competition in North America." Established in 1855, it's the place where wineries have their carefully crafted pedigrees validated, or refuted. So how could a discount wine like the Charles Shaw Chardonnay not only compete with, but best so many far more expensive wines?

They changed the game.

Charles Shaw winemaker Fred Franzia democratized fine wines by focusing on stridently pragmatic operations. His bottling plant was a model of production efficiency tucked into an industrial-looking area near Modesto, California, which is located more than one hundred miles from the windswept estuarine flats that are home to the genteel vineyards of Napa Valley. When asked how he competes, his answer was simple, elegant, and maddening to the much larger brands he competes against. "We choose to sell good quality wines at $2 a bottle because we think it's a fair price," Franzia said in an ABC News story, adding, "We think the other people are charging too much!"[1]

⬦⬦⬦⬦⬦

WHAT DEFINES A CHALLENGER BRAND?

As we saw in Chapter One, there are challenger stories all around us. In wine, sports, entertainment, politics, society—in virtually any competitive environment you can think of. The corporate world is no different, and in fact, offers the grandest, most diverse playing field there is for challengers and underdogs.

According to the most recent U.S. Census information from

the Small Business Association, in 2010, there were 27.9 million small businesses in the U.S. and 18,500 firms with five hundred employees or more.[2] Take out the top dogs in each of those sectors of business and that leaves a lot of underdogs nipping at their heels trying to compete. Look around and you'll see challenger brands of every size and type in every single category. Does that mean every brand not in first place is a challenger brand? No. But they could be.

From our experience over thirty years, there are three primary factors that distinguish true challenger brands from the leading brands in their categories. In his book, *Eating The Big Fish*, marketing strategist Adam Morgan identifies two of these factors as "state of market" and "state of mind."[3] To those, we add a third we call "state of readiness."

STATE OF MARKET

State of market refers to a company's position in the marketplace, or more specifically, its position in its category. In the more than $62 billion U.S. wine business[4], Charles Shaw is far from the best-selling Chardonnay in terms of units sold. And selling at just $2 per bottle, in 2007, the company wasn't leading the pack with respect to revenue generation.

Challenger brands are never traditional category leaders. They may be large companies in their own right, but number one they are not. Franzia has sold more than half a billion bottles of Charles Shaw Chardonnay, but they are not the biggest fish in their pond. What they are is a brand with a culture of ambition. Challenger brands like Charles Shaw don't enjoy the seemingly endless resources of category leaders. Instead, they choose to outthink their competition rather than outspend them. Every successful challenger brand has to have an extremely good understanding of where they stand in the market. Only then can they take advantage of not being the big dog everyone else is chasing.

STATE OF MIND

State of mind refers to a company's understanding of who they are. Challenger brands are either the best at delivering something important to a specific group of customers, or they are actively striving to become the best at delivering something their customers want. Now, thirteen years after their win at the State Fair, Charles Shaw is still one of the best at delivering a very inexpensive bottle of premium quality Chardonnay. In the past decade, other brands like Yellowtail and Barefoot have successfully joined that space with more brands showing up every month. But in 2007, nobody delivered affordable quality better than Charles Shaw as verified by the impartial judges at the California State Fair Wine Competition. And yet, their immediate reaction to schooling Napa Valley was not to quadruple protection, or to expand distribution from Trader Joe's to every grocery store from California to Maine. Charles Shaw knew who they were and, in great part, that's why they are still excellent. Challenger brands share a culture of commitment, and their organizational orientation toward excellence cannot be overstated.

STATE OF READINESS

The final challenger brand distinction is perhaps the most important of the three. State of readiness refers to how prepared a company is to go to battle. You can know where you stand and who you are, but without the readiness and willingness to act, compete, take a chance, and move forward, you might as well be paralyzed. True challenger brands engender a corporate culture of willingness, an openness and an energy for embracing new modes of thinking. This includes a higher organizational tolerance for calculated risk-taking. Often, this culture is present early in a company's life cycle but may wane as the company matures, and modes of thinking become traditionalized. It can be reignited during an organizational inflection point, such as a leadership change, or a reengineering process that has been intentionally and effectively managed. But regardless of origin, the company's collective mindset must embrace alternative ideas.

Again, consider Charles Shaw. Instead of following the practices of his competitors in Napa Valley, Fred Franzia organized his company around a more industrialized model that prized efficiency and speed over mystique and tradition. In essence, Franzia rewrote the rules of the industry so his company could win. That is the quintessential challenger brand move. Before Starbucks was Starbucks, it was a single coffee shop in Seattle. Not so many years ago, Tesla was a figment of Elon Musk's imagination. Chick-fil-A was a mall food court mainstay that only sold chicken sandwiches. Just a little more than a decade ago, the iPhone didn't exist. To paraphrase Apple's wonderful "Think Different" commercial from a few years back, the companies that are willing to take calculated risks and believe they can change the world are the ones who do.

THE IMPORTANCE OF CULTURE

Later in the book, we'll look at the importance of culture in detail. But at this point, it is useful to elaborate briefly on the corporate culture necessary for fostering challenger brands. We call it the "challenger culture" because it is typical of challenger organizations. While there is great variety in corporate cultures even among challengers, in our experience, challenger brands share some important cultural traits that allow them to punch above their weight including an organizational commitment to excellence, purposeful ambition, and most importantly, a pervasive sense of willingness. These are the traits that feed a company's state of mind and state of readiness. But they are just the beginning.

∞∞∞∞∞

ADVERTISING THE CHALLENGER BRAND

Being a challenger brand and *selling* a challenger brand are two different issues. Marketing and advertising challenger brands require significant leverage of a company's state of mind and state of readiness in a manner that changes the environment to the advantage of the challenger. In other words, it's not enough to simply talk the challenger language or even employ some challenger tactics. Truly successful challenger brands live and breathe in a culture steeped in the challenger orientation until it simply becomes part of who they are.

To build that culture, there are four things every challenger brand must have:

A CHALLENGER STRATEGY

Challenger brands must devise a marketing strategy that challenges category conventions and does not simply mimic the moves of the leader or other successful category competitors. Often, the marketing strategy is rooted in a business strategy built around challenging conventional category thinking, as in the case of Charles Shaw. Fred Franzia didn't try to out-Napa Napa. He conceived and executed an entirely different business model than his competitors were using to find one that worked for him.

Leadership teams for authentic challenger brands like Charles Shaw evaluate the competitive landscape with an eye toward changing something fundamental about the way they approach the business. In doing so, they create a new and distinctive competitive advantage. When this is accomplished successfully, it creates a new and clear path for a unique marketing strategy. Franzia certainly could have marketed his Charles Shaw brand the way the category competitors did, but he would have missed a significant opportunity for category distinction.

CHALLENGER PROMISES

Challenger brands must also make brand promises that aren't easily duplicated by competitors. The promise must be solidly grounded in *real* differences created by the company's state of mind—something it does best or is striving earnestly to do best. This promise must be authentic. It cannot simply be manufactured through advertising. The authentic difference for the Charles Shaw brand is not that it is an award-winning Chardonnay. The distinction is the company's ability to sell it profitably for $2 a bottle, and its willingness—even desire—to do so. That distinction cannot be invented through marketing or advertising, although it creates a significant opportunity that can be leveraged strongly through clever marketing and advertising. Franzia was able to use this authentic difference to do something many challenger brands do— he created an entirely new category. This time, for wine.

CHALLENGER STATEMENT

Challenger brands must be willing to make clear and compelling statements about what they are and what they are not, who they are for and who they are not for. Famous challenger brands such as Red Bull, Southwest Airlines, and Motel 6 are very specific about what they have to offer and who they are for. They are also not afraid to position themselves clearly away from customer groups that aren't in their crosshairs. For instance, Red Bull is not for ladies having a soda over lunch. Southwest Airlines is not for people who like to fly first-class. Motel 6 most assuredly isn't for the traveler who wants something more than a clean room at a great price. And Two Buck Chuck clearly isn't aimed at pleasing wine connoisseurs who favor the traditional practices of mainstream California vineyards or take pride in spending $20, $30, $40, or much more for a good bottle of wine.

Challenger brands are not afraid to limit their appeal at the expense of alienating those who will merely tolerate them. They are laser focused on those who will love them. The benefit for the challenger brand is a fervently loyal core customer base.

A CHALLENGER VOICE

Challenger brands are willing to amplify their strategies, brand promises, and statements through a unique voice. Their advertising and marketing communications look and sound different from their competitors. They say different things, make different promises, and command a different kind of attention in the marketplace. The state of readiness extant in challenger brand leadership not only paves the way for unique and unconventional marketing and advertising, it compels them to seek it out.

∞∞∞∞∞

TEAMING UP WITH A MARKETING PARTNER

Challenger brands often don't recognize themselves as such. American business culture is consumed with leading and being first, and many companies don't readily recognize or appreciate the inherent advantages of a strongly positioned "following brand." Often, a marketing partner's first role is to help frame the context so client leadership recognizes itself as a challenger and begins to understand the significant power in that position. A discussion about the concepts described above serves as the starting point for clarifying the status of a company's state of market, state of mind, and state of readiness for tackling the market as a true challenger brand.

When evaluating a marketing partner to help develop and leverage a challenger brand plan, it is important to identify a company that also fully appreciates and embraces the challenger brand ethos. The firm's own culture should reflect the states of market, mind, and readiness exemplified by a challenger brand as articulated in this chapter. Remember, it's not about speaking the challenger language. It's about living it. If you're in a place where you need a marketing partner, look for a firm that has the disposition and specific tools and processes in place for developing a challenger plan from beginning to end. For themselves, and for you.

○○○○○○

FOOTNOTES

[1] "California's Wine Surprise," by ABC News. July 12, 2007.

[2] "Frequently Asked Questions About Small Business," Small Business Association (SBA) Office of Advocacy, Sept., 2012.

[3] Adam Morgan, *Eating The Big Fish: How Challenger Brands Can Compete Against Brand Leaders*, (Hoboken, NJ: John WIley & Sons, 2009); 26.

[4] Liz Thach, "Overview of the US Wine Industry in 2018: Stable Growth Forecasted – Based on 2017 Stats," Dr. Liz Thach, MW, Jan. 31, 2018.

3

WHY CHALLENGER BRANDS
ARE HARD TO BEAT

In Chapter One, we listed a number of compelling reasons why people love underdogs and challenger brands. But being loved and being successful aren't always the same thing. We love Charlie Brown, but he still never gets to kick the football.

For challenger brands, achieving any level of success is an uphill climb. But actually competing with and winning against category leaders with more money, more resources, and more time? That's next to impossible. Or so you would think.

The truth is, great challenger brands are remarkably resilient. Pepsi was started in 1898, just six years after the invention of Coca-Cola. Avis was started in 1946. Burger King in 1954. Volkswagen was started in 1937 in Berlin and then marketed to Americans fifteen years after we put an end to Germany's quest for world domination. Talk about an uphill climb.

For every Ford, there's a Chevy. For every Starbucks, there's a Dunkin' Donuts. For every Nike, there's a Reebok… and an Adidas, a Puma, a New Balance, an ASICS, an Under Armour, an Avia, a

Saucony, and a Skechers. It stands to reason that every category leader will have competition along the way and at the same time, it's kind of shocking that so many challengers survive. It's like a massive, centuries-long game of RISK with brands instead of countries, and the little guys just keep rolling sixes.

Look at the soft drink industry. You would think that in 120 years, Coca-Cola would have had enough money, media, and leadership to wipe Pepsi, Dr Pepper, RC, and the others off the map. Coke is the biggest brand in the world. And yet, they haven't been able to do it. Not even close.

Old or new, large or small, underdogs find a way to survive. It's part of their nature. And in way more instances than you might think, challenger brands find a way to win. That's not to say there aren't numerous disadvantages to being the little guy. There are. But there are also a number of surprising advantages to being an underdog. A dozen to be exact. The key is understanding what they are and leveraging them for success.

Recall what we discussed in Chapter Two regarding "state of mind," "state of market," and "state of readiness." As Socrates was fond of saying, "First, know thyself," and that couldn't be truer for brands going into battle. If you want to succeed as a challenger, you must first understand who you are, where you fit, and how prepared you are to compete. Once those things are clear, you can lean into these twelve advantages and leverage them to the hilt in your quest to take down the category giants.

◇◇◇◇◇◇

12 SURPRISING ADVANTAGES
OF BEING A CHALLENGER

1. EVERYONE PULLS FOR THE CHALLENGER

In Chapter One, we talked about how, as human beings, something deep inside us is hard-wired to root for the underdog. And when the narrative includes a notion of redemption, or overcoming overwhelming odds, we root even harder. Consider the coverage of Tiger Woods winning the 2019 Masters. It had been eleven years since his last victory in a Major. Eleven years filled with erratic behavior, divorce, physical decline, multiple back surgeries, endless criticism, and overwhelming doubt as to whether Tiger would ever be competitive again, let alone win. And yet on Sunday, April 14, 2019, there was Tiger, standing in Butler Cabin after an epic comeback on the back nine, receiving his fifth Masters green jacket with the world—not just the sports world, the whole world—buzzing with an excitement we hadn't seen since 1997, when Tiger crushed the field by winning his first Masters by twelve strokes.

Smart challenger brands understand the masses are rooting for them to succeed, and they leverage that by giving consumers an emotional reason to connect. Consider the origin story from the website of eyeglass upstart Warby Parker:

> *"Every idea starts with a problem. Ours was simple: glasses are too expensive. We were students when one of us lost his glasses on a backpacking trip. The cost of replacing them was so high that he spent the first semester of grad school without them, squinting and complaining. (We don't*

recommend this.) The rest of us had similar experiences, and we were amazed at how hard it was to find a pair of great frames that didn't leave our wallets bare. Where were the options?

It turns out there was a simple explanation. The eyewear industry is dominated by a single company that has been able to keep prices artificially high while reaping huge profits from consumers who have no other options.

We started Warby Parker to create an alternative."[1]

Who wouldn't cheer for that company? Nobody likes a bully and here are two poor grad students taking on Goliath on behalf of glasses wearers everywhere. Once upon a time, that would have been a great story, but one that was difficult for people to actively support. But not anymore. With the dawn of the digital age, the barriers to supporting smaller challenger brands have been removed. It doesn't matter that there isn't a brick and mortar Warby Parker store near my house. I have a phone and a credit card. All I have to do is walk to the mailbox.

A few years ago, an episode of "Shark Tank" featured a company called Three Jerks that made beef jerky out of Filet Mignon. It looked delicious, and the sharks went nuts for it. Before the show had even ended, we Googled the company, found their website and tried to place an order. They were already sold out. For months. That's amazing. But it's not unique to them. In the ten years "Shark Tank" has been on the air, they've helped hundreds of upstarts and underdogs make millions and millions of dollars and achieve unprecedented success. It's the combination of a great idea, the right exposure, and our collective desire to see the little guys succeed. In them, we see a little piece of ourselves and we know that if that was *our* idea on the line, we'd sure want people supporting us.

2. COMPETITORS UNDERESTIMATE CHALLENGERS

Call it overconfidence, misinformation, or hubris on the part of those at the top of the food chain, but one of the great advantages to being an underdog is that competitors, and especially category leaders, almost always underestimate you. They can't help it. When you're on top, it feels like the world is yours and that you get to dictate the rules of play. There's an ever present "We're Number One" confidence that infuses everything. But what leaders forget is that while they're catching their breath from reaching the summit, or resting on their laurels, their challengers are doubling their efforts to figure out how to bring them down.

Brand leaders, in fact, often fail to acknowledge the real threats posed by their smaller competitors until those threats are knocking on the door catching them completely by surprise. Historically, it's in that moment when companies make really bad decisions in response. It even happened to the biggest brand in the world.

After a century of domination, in the early 1980s, Coca-Cola found itself suddenly losing ground to Pepsi, in large part because of the "Pepsi Challenge" ad campaign. Rather than address the marketing, Coca-Cola did the unthinkable. They changed the formula and launched a sweeter, more Pepsi-like version called

"New Coke" in 1985. It was a disaster and literally within weeks, Coke pulled "New Coke" off the shelves and reverted back to the original formula rebranded as "Coca-Cola Classic." Many consider it the greatest blunder in branding history. Roger Enrico, then the chairman of Pepsi, wrote a fantastic book about the whole episode called *The Other Guy Blinked* (1986), and that's exactly what happened. Coke underestimated Pepsi's effect on their brand until they finally decided to respond, and when they did, they underestimated themselves. They completely forgot who they were. Their only saving grace was their willingness to admit the mistake quickly and fix it.

3. IT'S EASIER FOR CHALLENGERS TO FLY UNDER THE RADAR

Corollary to big brands underestimating challenger brands is the ability of smaller companies to fly under the radar. How many times have you discovered a "new" company, either on your own, or on someone else's recommendation, only to find it's a huge deal?

Long before they were part of the national consciousness, Uber, Camp Gladiator, and Airbnb were methodically and systematically going about their business, converting new fans and quietly (at first) disrupting everything we know about transportation, gyms, and hotels. They were simultaneously small companies and huge underdogs trying to crack their way into some of the most difficult, competitive, expensive categories there are, and they won by doing things so completely differently from their competitors that no one paid any attention. Their "state of readiness" wasn't, "How do we win the game?" It was, "How do we change it?"

Cabs are dirty, expensive, and never where you need them to be. What if we empowered drivers to work on their schedules, use their own cars, and work where they live?

Gyms are expensive to build, expensive to join, and require a big population to support the overhead. What if we delivered a fun, rigorous, positive workout experience, but without the gym?

The hotel business is huge, complex, and incredibly expensive to get into and maintain. What if we created a network of "owners" who used their own homes for lodging? An instant, global lodging empire without ever having to lay a single brick.

Today, the fastest growing "cab" company in the world doesn't own a cab. The fastest growing workout brand in the country doesn't own a gym. The fastest growing hospitality company on the planet doesn't own a hotel. Uber, Camp Gladiator, and Airbnb are what it looks like to fly under the radar when your competitors aren't looking or even paying attention. If you're a challenger brand, understand that opportunity for what it is and take advantage of it.

4. CHALLENGERS CAN BE MORE NIMBLE

According to Newton's First Law of Motion, the bigger and heavier an object is, the harder it is to move. In other words, if the Titanic had been a bass boat, the iceberg wouldn't have been a problem. The same goes for brands. Often, the bigger they are, the more difficult they are to maneuver. More offices, more people, and more management levels require more effort, more planning, and more time. By contrast, smaller brands have less of everything and should be able to move much faster.

Let's say lightning strikes and your brand team identifies a fantastic opportunity, but time is of the essence. (When is it not in the advertising and marketing world?) In a big organization with a big brand agency, you're looking at multiple levels of approval, the time to write a creative brief, back and forth on internal approvals, and at the agency, time for a briefing, time for the creative team to work their magic, time for a round or two of revisions, time for production, time for... zzzzzzzz.

Meanwhile, the underdog brand has everyone in a room stocked with Blue Moons and Rolos discussing the opportunity, concepting solutions, and planning the production before the first mid-level manager at Big Brand sends her revisions back on the first round of the creative brief.

Being small can be a big disadvantage when it comes to things like manpower and cash flow. But it can also be a *huge* advantage when it comes to moving quickly. If you're small and not moving nimbly, something is wrong. Figure out what it is, and fix it. Look at any situation where David beat Goliath, and you can be sure swiftness and agility played a role.

5. IT'S EASIER FOR CHALLENGERS TO BUILD, ADAPT, AND MAINTAIN THEIR CULTURES

We're going to get to the importance of extraordinary culture and how to build one in later chapters, but for now, let's just agree that building and maintaining an authentic, inclusive, sustainable culture is crucial to the success of your company and your brand.

More often than not, uber-successful brands have and maintain a distinctive culture. They know who they are, and they live into that identity on a daily basis. Think Apple. Pixar. Chick-fil-A.

Whole Foods. Those companies are four of the biggest disruptors in history, and each one has a culture that's envied by companies everywhere. And here's the secret: They didn't build the company and then create the culture. It was there from the beginning. That's not to say their cultures didn't evolve. Apple certainly had its share of bumps before "thinking differently" when Steve Jobs was rehired, but Apple's culture has always been about the marriage of design and tech while facilitating creativity. From the first location in the first mall food court, Chick-fil-A prided themselves on delivering exceptional food and unprecedented service. That has never wavered.

Because of their size and because of their concentrated leadership, it's easier for challenger brands to build, adapt, and maintain their cultures. Too often, it's an afterthought. But for those with the vision and discipline to build their culture side-by-side with their brand from the beginning, there are advantages that simply cannot be manufactured on demand. Define your culture. Build it. Hire the right people into that culture, and train them to be custodians and protectors of it. When you have that kind of buy-in—when your team owns its culture—your organizational strength is exponential.

6. CHALLENGERS REMEMBER HOW TO HUSTLE

There's an old English proverb that states, "Necessity is the mother of invention." It didn't originate with challenger brands, but it could have. One of the core tenets of challenger brands is that they find a way where there is no way. Underdogs are fighters. They're tenacious. They don't give up. The Greatest Generation called that "hustle" and it's a concept most challengers are intimately familiar with.

Because challenger brands don't have the budgets and resources that category leaders do, they are forced to achieve more with less. That starts with smarter strategies and better creative work, but it also means making the most of the resources at your disposal.

Over the past twenty years here at LOOMIS, we've noticed that advertising and marketing people tend to be fairly complex, educated, accomplished individuals with hidden talents and myriad experiences. On more than a few (dozen) occasions, we've been able to tap those talents to do things in-house that could have cost us thousands of dollars. What secret talents are hidden among your staff like buried treasure? Are there singers? Actors? Artists? Musicians? Are there people with expertise in a given intellectual area? Are there folks who can build things, or who know people who can?

Hustling means looking around you and harnessing the resources at your disposal. It's easy when you can buy everything you need. But often, the easiest solution isn't the best solution. When you have to hustle for something, it makes you want it and appreciate it that much more.

7. CHALLENGERS OFTEN HAVE MORE CONSOLIDATED LEADERSHIP

While not an absolute, more often than not, challengers tend to have more consolidated leadership than category leaders. When that leadership is strong, it can be a huge advantage. With every layer of leadership comes a need for more time, more communication, and more coordination to get anything done. Not only that, every layer of leadership puts employees one step farther away from the brand leaders at the top.

Think about the difference between a gargantuan movie studio like Disney and the much smaller Pixar, one of the studios they own. Due to its sheer size (Disney is a $59 billion company that employs more than 201,000 people), the House of Mouse has no choice but to build in layers of management to accommodate its division of labor. While efficient, every layer puts more and more people farther and farther away from Chairman Bob Chapek and the visionary leadership at the top. Contrast that with Pixar which allows employees at all levels to view films in progress and provide input to the directors and animators. When you have 1,200 people like Pixar—and even that's a big company—you can maintain a sense of cultural intimacy and give every employee a feeling of connection to leadership at the top.

It's not that smaller works and bigger fails. It's simply a different dynamic requiring a different kind of leadership. Where the advantage lies for challenger brands is that smaller makes it easier to engage your people on a personal level. To help them see and understand the vision for your brand. To make them feel part of something special and bigger than themselves. The challengers who fly are the ones with smart, humble, passionate leaders who take advantage of their size by engaging their people personally. Not once a year at some company meeting, once a week, or even once a day. But who inspire, motivate, and calibrate their cultural alignment as often as they can.

8. CHALLENGERS CAN GO WHERE BIG BRANDS CAN'T, OR WON'T

One of the most fascinating aspects about challenger brands is that they often go where big brands either can't or won't. Part of that is due to the sheer size of category leaders. Some of it is due to their mindsets, a reduced appetite for risk, or the fear of what taking chances might do to the stock price on Wall Street. Truthfully, there are dozens of reasons why big companies tend to be safe, stodgy, and sedentary. And while you can justify all of them, those rationales also open the door for underdogs who are willing to take a chance. Think Apple leaning into home computing when IBM wouldn't. Or Zappos selling shoes through the mail.

If you work in any facet of advertising and marketing, you've most likely heard the cautionary tale about Netflix and the demise of Blockbuster. (For those born after the year 2000, there was a time when, if you wanted to watch a movie, you had to get in the car and drive to a video store to rent a VHS tape, or later, a DVD. You kept it for two or three days and then returned it, usually owing an exorbitant late fee because you forgot and returned it late. Or didn't rewind the tape. That store was called Blockbuster.)

From its founding in 1985 through its rapid ascent to more than 2,800 brick-and-mortar stores worldwide, Blockbuster was the eight-hundred-pound gorilla of movie rentals. Every town had one and they were one of America's most ubiquitous brands. In less than a decade, Blockbuster's valuation went from $0 to $8.4 billion. But times, they were a–changing.

In 1997, two software engineers named Reed Hastings and Marc Randolph started a company called Netflix. For a monthly subscription, Netflix would send customers DVDs through the mail with no late fees. You just watched when you wanted and mailed it back in a Netflix-supplied sleeve. And as technology and people's digital capabilities caught up, Netflix shifted mainly to a streaming model. In 2000, Hastings approached Blockbuster about a merger for $50 million that would put his team in charge of Blockbuster's online rental program. Blockbuster declined. They were certain there was no way the Netflix model could beat people's love for their neighborhood Blockbuster down the street.

By 2004, Blockbuster's market valuation declined to $6 billion while Netflix was still climbing past $500 million. Five years later, Blockbuster had lost a third of its value, while Netflix was about to crest $2 billion. A year later in 2010, Blockbuster declared bankruptcy. Call it really poor management. Call it hubris. Call it lack of vision. We think it was all three. Blockbuster could have been Netflix. Even after Netflix was Netflix. But their unwillingness to embrace change and believe there could be something better killed them.

As of this writing, Netflix has a market cap somewhere north of $167 billion. It offers customers access to more than 5,500 movies and TV shows, all for as little as $7.95 a month. It has been ranked as the most valuable entertainment company in the world, and, in February 2019, it had an original film called "Roma" that garnered ten Academy Award nominations including Best Picture. In 2020, they had two Best Picture contenders with "The Irishman" and "Marriage Story" that garnered sixteen Oscar nominations between them.

Netflix continues to rewrite the entertainment landscape and all because they were willing to go where the category leader wouldn't. What opportunities are lying right in front of you now?

9. CHALLENGERS ATTRACT TALENT WHO WANT TO MAKE A DIFFERENCE

One of our favorite business books is a book by Simon Sinek called *Start with Why* (2011). In it, he explains that great and inspiring companies understand not just what they do, but why they do it. In a companion TED Talk on YouTube, Sinek describes it this way:

> *"Every single person, every single organization on the planet knows what they do. One hundred percent. Some, know how they do it. Whether you call it your differentiating value proposition, or your proprietary process, or USP. But very, very few people or organizations know why they do what they do. And by why, I don't mean to make a profit. That's a result. It's always a result. By why, I mean what's your purpose? What's your cause? What's your belief? Why does your organization exist?"[2]*

Sinek illustrates that most companies think from the outside in—what, how, why—but that the inspired companies start with "why" and work their way out. He then uses Apple as an example:

> *"If Apple were like everyone else, a marketing message from them might sound like this: 'We make great computers. They're beautifully designed, easy to use and user friendly.*

Want to buy one?' Meh. And that's how most of us communicate. That's how most marketing is done, how most sales is done. And that's how most of us communicate interpersonally. We say what we do. We say how we're different or how we're better and we expect some sort of behavior. A purchase, a vote, or something like that. 'Here's our new law firm. We have the best lawyers with the biggest clients. We always perform. Do business with us. Here's our new car. It gets great mileage, it has leather seats. Buy our car.' But it's uninspiring.

Here's how Apple actually communicates: 'Everything we do, we believe in challenging the status quo. We believe in thinking differently. The way we challenge the status quo is by making our products beautifully designed, simple to use, and user friendly. We just happen to make great computers. Want to buy one?'

Totally different, right? People don't buy what you do, they buy why you do it".[2]

We tell that story because it speaks to the talent who are drawn to challenger brand thinking and challenger brand companies. Challenger brands are all about questioning the status quo, thinking differently, and changing the world. Which do you think sounds more appealing to great thinkers, innovative leaders, and people with the kind of mindset you need to go after the category leaders? The disruptive upstart company looking for innovative thinking and new paths, or the established leader who's just fine doing things the way they've always been done? Challenger brands attract people who want to make a difference and who want to make an impact, but only if that's the kind of company you are authentically from your core to your culture.

10. CHALLENGERS HAVE A "CHANGE THE GAME" MINDSET

One of the greatest commercials that has ever run (from one of the greatest campaigns) was a 1997 Apple commercial created by TBWA\Chiat\Day called "Think Different." In it, over a montage of the world's most innovative thinkers and artists from Einstein to Gandhi to MLK to Picasso to Jim Henson, a voiceover says:

> *"Here's to the crazy ones. The misfits. The rebels. The troublemakers. The round pegs in the square holes. The ones who see things differently. They're not fond of rules and have no respect for the status quo. You can quote them, disagree with them, glorify, or vilify them. About the only thing you can't do is ignore them. Because they change things. They push the human race forward. And while some may see them as the crazy ones, we see genius. Because the people who are crazy enough to think they can change the world, are the ones who do".[3]*

It's no shock that this spot came from one of the great challenger brands of all time, or that it was Apple (and their agency's brilliant creative team) who so beautifully articulated what it is that sets underdogs apart from the rest of the pack. Great challenger brands don't sit around thinking of ways to win the game. They think about ways to change it. David didn't look for a better way to grapple with Goliath or for a sneakier way to fight up close. He examined his opponent's strengths and found a way to use his gifts that was so lethal and unexpected that the Philistine never saw the rock coming until it smacked him between the eyes.

If you're a challenger and you're stuck playing your competitors' games, you're missing out on one of your key advantages. Find your way to break the mold and then commit to it. There's a reason the word disruption is a favored word among strong challenger brands.

11. FOR CHALLENGERS, TIME IS OF THE ESSENCE

When you lack unlimited resources, you can't afford to sit around and take your time with things. When you're the underdog, it's always "Go Time!" And while that may tend to amp you up a bit, make no mistake—a real sense of urgency can be a big advantage. Adrenaline is a good thing. Our fathers liked to call it "lighting a fire under your ass." Whichever you prefer, moving with a sense of urgency and purpose can energize your whole team. Especially if you're the one leading the way.

As much as we may not want to admit it, folks who work for us tack off of our behavior, our moods, our energy, and our excitement. If we're all in, they will be, too. And as the underdog, we don't have forever. Our competitors are too big, too well compensated and have too many resources. They can wait us out, buy us out, or smoke us out, and if we're content to sit back and watch, there's little we can do about it. But what if that's not our mindset? What if instead, we chose to be brave and take our swings no matter the outcome?

Challengers have to lean into a mindset of commitment. A mindset to make a decision and see it through, whatever the result. We can't afford not to. Andy Andrews, renowned speaker and best-selling author of *The Seven Decisions* and *The Traveler's Gift*, addresses this very thing. He says, "Intention without action is an insult to those who expect the best from you." For challengers, time is of the essence. If you really want to go after the leaders, stop dreaming, and start disrupting. So what if you fail? Get back up and swing harder. To paraphrase poet Alfred, Lord Tennyson, it is far better—far more satisfying—to have tried and failed, than never to have tried at all.

12. NO ONE EXPECTS CHALLENGERS TO WIN

Years ago for our birthdays, one of our dearest friends gave us decorative steel blocks for our desks that say, "What would you do if you knew you could not fail?" Let's be honest. Nobody expects the underdog to win. As spectators, we hope for it, we root for it, and we cheer for it. But in our hearts, we know it's probably not going to happen. The same is true when our competitors look at us. They'll pat us on the head. They'll acknowledge we're in the game. They might even pay attention to what we're doing from time to time. But they're not sweating a hostile takeover. And that's right where we want them.

As an underdog, one of your greatest advantages is being underestimated. Ask Buster Douglas. Rulon Gardner. The UMBC Men's basketball team. Ask President Trump. In sports, we talk about teams "playing loose," or "not playing tight." In essence, playing like they cannot fail. When they so choose, challenger brands can take advantage of the same energy. Work hard. Be smart. Leave it all on the court and be good with whatever happens.

◇◇◇◇◇◇◇

FOOTNOTES

[1] www.warbyparker.com/history

[2] Simon Sinek, "Start With Why – how great leaders inspire action | Simon Sinek | TEDxPugetSound," Sept. 28, 2009, YouTube.

[3] Apple - Here's to the Crazy Ones (1997), May 23, 2010, YouTube.

4

⬦⬦⬦⬦⬦

WHEN BRAND MEETS CULTURE

Orit Gadiesh pulls no punches. The Chairman of Bain & Company is an imposing intellectual whose command of both logic and emotion are paired with a matching command of any stage where she's a featured speaker. Her resume includes a psychology degree from Harvard, an MBA from Brown, a faculty position at The Hebrew University's Jerusalem Institute of Management, and service in the Israeli Army. She's appeared on *Forbes'* list of the world's most powerful women four times. She's also one of the world's foremost authorities on corporate change.

People pay attention to what Gadiesh has to say, and when she told a room full of CEOs who they should blame when a warm meal is served cold, they listened carefully. We've all had a poorly prepared meal at a restaurant, she explained. The impulsive response is to blame the servers or the kitchen staff and, while that may not be entirely wrong, it's not entirely right, either. Blaming the staff misses a much larger and far more important point, she told them. Ultimately, Gadiesh intoned, it is the restaurant's culture that informs the behavior of the staff.

Something about the culture of the restaurant tells the waiter, who no doubt knows when a dish is poorly prepared, to serve it to the customer rather than push back on the kitchen to get it right. It's the restaurant's culture that signals what is acceptable and unacceptable behavior, either overtly or—more often—through things left unsaid. What's more, the restaurant's culture, like that of any organization, is a direct reflection of its leadership. The values of leaders are communicated by their behavior and transmitted through relationships. Intentional or otherwise, the way leaders lead tells a group all it needs to know about how to behave.

When a restaurant serves a warm meal cold, more often than not, it's no simple mistake. Instead, it's the restaurant's unmistakable culture that allowed it to happen at all, and the restaurant's leader is responsible for shaping that culture. Blame for a dish served cold is most correctly assigned to the restaurant's owner, head chef, or whoever established the restaurant's standards and vision for customer experience.

CULTURE STARTS AT THE TOP

What does a bad meal have to do with the leader of JPMorgan Chase and the bank's behavior during the housing crisis of 2008? Gadiesh shared this restaurant anecdote during a talk she gave in 2009 as the nation wobbled under the weight of the worst recession since the Great Depression. The world was gripped by a global financial crisis catalyzed in the United States by the subprime mortgage meltdown, and then compounded by a number of factors whose unfortunate combination delivered devastating financial blows to millions of Americans who lost jobs, savings, homes, hopes, and dreams.

While it might be useful to know who to summon the next time dinner out goes badly, the question posed to Gadiesh was far more serious than that. She had been asked whether Chase Chairman and CEO Jamie Dimon was personally responsible for the actions of subordinates who were accused of knowingly underwriting fraudulent securities. The room was full of somber business leaders who were still making sense of a newly emerging counter-narrative about the banking stalwart and its principled leader.

Chase was positioned as the vanguard of an industry under siege. The international banking giant had long been heralded as the lone white hat bank that, unlike all their Wall Street peers, hadn't done anything wrong. Chase was the last bank standing after sidestepping the historic credit crisis under Dimon's canny and charismatic leadership. More than anything, it seemed he had led with integrity where others had failed to lead at all.

Desired or not, Jamie Dimon was cast as the wartime General of the banking industry, and Wall Street was grateful. Everyone was grateful. At this particular moment in the history of America's most significant financial brands, the brilliance of the Chase brand was eclipsed only by the shiny virtue of Dimon's personal brand.

As the financial crisis unfolded, Chase had become widely regarded as the North Star in an absolute mess of a constellation. Wall Street needed a savior, and it had one in Dimon when he marshalled Chase to the rescue of both Bear Stearns and Washington Mutual. It was the stuff of heroes after the breathtaking demise of a series of luminous financial industry brands, including Goldman Sachs, Morgan Stanley, Merrill Lynch, and Lehman Brothers. The world, and more specifically the American economy, couldn't take much more. In a retrospective piece some five years after the collapse, Vanity Fair described Dimon's rescue of Bear Stearns and Washington Mutual as an act of "financial patriotism that certainly helped prevent the U.S. economy from further doubling over on itself."[1] And yet Chase was not without fault.

Given the backdrop of an economy in freefall and relentless headlines about big banks behaving badly, it didn't take much to arouse a little anxiety in a room filled with business leaders. A simple question to Gadiesh did the trick: was Dimon responsible for the behavior of his employees? He had offered ignorance as his alibi, after all, claiming he was simply unaware of the fraud being perpetrated by subordinates in his bank.

It was perhaps the very lionizing of Dimon which provoked Gadiesh to begin gently with a benign example about a poorly served meal at a restaurant, but the trajectory of her answer was clear soon enough. Her position was unambiguous as she noted that the Chase culture, while perhaps well concealed from public view, most certainly promoted behaviors conducive to a fraudulent and deceptive scheme to sell mortgage-backed securities loaded with defective loans. Dimon may have been the protagonist in a badly needed Wall Street hero's journey, but that most certainly did not exonerate him. Dimon was responsible for his company's behavior.

In the end, Chase settled with federal and state authorities for a record-setting $13 billion in fines. As it turned out, in an industry made rotten by an industry-wide culture that fostered environments of predatory opportunism, Chase was simply no exception. With six- and seven-figure bonuses as their prize, big bank employees pursued personal fortune with reckless abandon and with no regard whatsoever for the law or for the dire consequences to be paid by their fellow Americans.

CULTURE IS POWERFUL. SO IS THE PERCEPTION OF IT. A decade hence, the big bank brands remain indelibly damaged by their deeds. Where trust and fidelity were once synonymous with America's major financial institutions, consumer suspicion and a lingering sense of betrayal are attached to them now. While the big banks are awash in cash today, all the money in the world cannot buy back the industry's integrity. It's a stubborn residue that will not be cleansed anytime soon by polished ad campaigns and outsized big bank marketing budgets. When push comes to shove, a company's culture is far more powerful than its brand.

Culture is also very durable and impossible to shift without serious intention and the will to match. In 2016, just seven years after a banking crisis that's estimated to have cost every American $70,000, Wells Fargo was embroiled in a scandal borne of the same malicious cultural cues. Top-down pressure to generate fee income motivated Wells employees to open millions of fraudulent savings and checking accounts on behalf of customers without their consent.

Culture is durable, indeed.

∞∞∞∞∞

BRANDS ARE FEELINGS

What does a company's culture have to do with its brand? In a word, everything. From the stage of a client conference, author Joe Calloway issued an excellent summary explanation for what a brand is, if only for its absolute coherence and elegant simplicity. His take: your brand is what people think it's like to do business with you.

Indeed, a brand is exactly that, and of course, brands are so much more. In fact, brands are meaning-making systems designed to reflect, signal, and communicate our values. The better they accomplish this, the more tightly aligned brands can become with our sense of personal identity.

For the purposes of evaluating our own brands and considering their performance, however, Calloway's take is awfully handy. Indeed, everything a company does in the service of advancing its brand rolls up into the way it makes people feel about doing business with them. How do people feel about doing business with big banks today? Perennial neo-banker Anthony Thompson shared his thoughts with *Forbes* a decade after the banking crisis:

> *The banking industry drones on about having to restore customers' trust in financial services—customers should have a healthy level of distrust of financial services in general and banks in particular. Many banks have ripped customers off, and in some instances, left the taxpayer holding the bill – it is a bank's primary job to manage distrust.*[2]

Thompson's take isn't at all surprising to anyone who has been paying attention. Many consumers generally don't feel good about doing business with big banks anymore. People simply don't like the way they behave, and that behavior has everything to do with the way big banks make consumers feel. Big bank ad campaigns still promise fidelity and security, but promises ring hollow when what is said and what is done are incongruent. At the end of the day, it is the bank's behavior that informs the way people feel about doing business with them, and that feeling is the brand. So in this very important respect, the culture that drives a company's behavior cannot be separated from its brand. They may not always get along, but culture and brand are blood relatives of the first order.

◇◇◇◇◇◇

BETTER CULTURE, BETTER BRAND

Just like companies and people, industries have reputations, and the reputation of every industry forms an overlay of consumer perception that creates a critical backdrop for every company the industry includes. We call it a category overlay, which is essentially the way that category makes people feel. Sound familiar?

Category overlays function a lot like brands do, and just like a brand image, some category overlays help a lot while others don't offer anything resembling help at all. The computer industry is full of gadgets people love. You've probably got one in your pocket or your purse. People use them for everything from work to play to managing their relationships. Computers hold our curiosity with continuous improvement; memory gets bigger, the devices get faster, and predictably, prices drop over time. It's a happy circumstance that defines the space where favorite brands like Apple, Microsoft, Samsung, Sony, and Alienware play. In fact, the category overlay for the computer industry is so positive, it might even resemble a halo.

While the categorical wind is at the backs of these computer brands, it's no surprise that the opposite is true for the banking industry today. That certainly makes the job of branding a bank all the more challenging. It also makes the job one bank is doing with its brand so much more remarkable. While the big banks were busy making a mess of mortgages (and their industry by default), a much smaller community bank was busy sowing the cultural seeds for a banking brand of a very different kind.

First United Bank's story contains a challenger case study for using company culture to build a better brand. More than that, the bank's approach has delivered a competitive advantage every challenger brand should seek to create. Just as the personalities of people are difficult to mimic in any authentic or believable way, First United's culture drives distinctive organizational behavior that cannot be easily replicated by any of their competitors.

What's the single most effective way to differentiate your brand? Marketers think in terms of features and benefits, points of difference and unique selling propositions, but the most authentic brand positioning is firmly grounded in company culture that energizes all of those things.

Culture informs everything about the way products are built and services are delivered. Best of all, it's the one thing competitors can never replicate. That makes company culture the ultimate challenger brand advantage. Start with culture, get it right, and build a strong brand. When culture and brand are in strong strategic alignment, the world sits up and takes notice.

◇◇◇◇◇◇

BANKING ON DIFFERENCE

Greg Massey is the CEO of First United Bank, headquartered on Main Street in Durant, Oklahoma. The address alone is sufficient for identifying theirs as a subcategory of the larger banking industry. First United Bank is not a large national bank, and Massey is no Wall Street banker. First United is a community bank with branches throughout Oklahoma and in Texas, and Massey is a purpose-driven banker.

Catch him in full stride on stage at his annual stakeholder meeting and you'll hear much more about leading with love and creating meaningful impact than you will about interest rates or investments. That's because his leadership is driven by a personal purpose founded on faith and fortified by the belief that banks are uniquely positioned to facilitate far more than financial transactions. Transformative experiences for all the bank's stakeholders—from employees to customers—are what ignite Massey's passion for what's possible at First United. He's on a quest to build a bank capable of delivering transformative impact at every turn, and it's Massey's deeply personal sensibility about the good things a bank can do for people and their communities that drives him and his team.

When Greg Massey looked at all First United could become, he started with Why. His vision is informed and driven by an acute awareness that financial stress destroys lives. And when he shares his insights on banking with finance students at universities, his talks are less about money and more about marriage. He talks about the toll debt takes on families, the causative role of finances in divorce, and the responsibility bankers have to offer credit carefully because of it.

Whether he's addressing thousands, or giving an intimate talk to a small group, Massey speaks about financial challenges and the harm they inflict on people's lives in a manner and tone you might expect from a deeply concerned friend. It's this compassion for the people and the communities the bank serves that inspired the headline of his favorite First United billboard that reads, "Which is better—twice the house, or half the mortgage?" It's an unexpected sentiment in an industry that rewards head over heart, but one that's evident at every turn underpinning the bank's mission to help its customers with empathy and education.

Massey's leadership is characteristic of a small but growing group of companies led by conscious leaders who eschew personal ambition and individual accomplishment for personal growth and development as leaders. In fact, Massey is a highly engaged champion of the conscious capitalism movement described by its founder, Whole Foods CEO John Mackey, and co-author Raj Sisodia, in their best-selling book *Conscious Capitalism: Liberating the Heroic Spirit of Business*. The movement's mission is nothing short of elevating humanity through good business. It's a business philosophy that drives not only virtuous corporate behavior, but real results, too.

In his book *Firms of Endearment: How World-Class Companies Profit from Passion and Purpose*, Sisodia cites research demonstrating that consciously-led publicly traded companies outperformed the S&P 500 Index by a factor of 10.5 from 1996 to 2011. A Harvard Business Review of the book had this to say about the exceptional performance of consciously-led companies:

> "Conscious companies treat their stakeholders better. As a consequence, their suppliers are happier to do business with them. Employees are more engaged, productive, and likely to stay. These companies are more welcome in their communities and their customers are more satisfied and loyal. The most conscious companies give more, and they get more in return. The inescapable conclusion: it pays to care, widely, and deeply."[3]

These results hold up for First United Bank, whose annual growth rate compares to those high performers cited in *Firms of Endearment*. First United dramatically outpaces its banking industry peers whose forecast year-over-year growth hovers between one and two percent.

◇◇◇◇◇◇

CULTURE STARTS WITH LEADERSHIP

Nothing happens without conscious leadership and the culture it creates. For better or for worse, it's an inescapable fact that company leadership drives corporate culture. From the C-suite to church, school, and government, we look to our leaders for all the important social cues about how to conduct ourselves as we try to fit into the groups that fill our lives with meaning. The academic and popular business literature on the way culture influences organizational behavior is vast indeed. What's discussed much less often is the powerful advantage that accrues to those companies that understand how culture can be used to create truly extraordinary brand distinction.

The key is congruence, and it's the reason First United Bank's brand position can never be co-opted by Chase Bank—or any other competitor. When a company's brand is tightly aligned with its culture, the result is a powerfully attractive clarity of purpose that resonates deeply with customers. That resonance serves as the basis for what the author of the seminal work on challenger branding describes as a lighthouse identity.

In *Eating the Big Fish*, Adam Morgan describes this as the kind of identity that's so radiantly clear that consumers use it to navigate the category.[4] It becomes the very basis for comparison among its competitive set and often more broadly. Think Starbucks, Apple, and Dove. The basis for the kind of brand and cultural congruence that allows a brand to shine the way they do can always be mapped back to the way a company's employees behave. Remember, your brand is what people think it's like to do business with you.

◇◇◇◇◇◇

FOOTNOTES

[1] William D. Cohan, "Jamie Dimon's $13 Billion Secret—Revealed," *Vanity Fair*, Sept. 6, 2017.

[2] Lawrence Wintermeyer, "Consumers Should not Trust Banks," *Forbes*, Sept. 20, 2018.

[3] Tony Schwartz, "Companies that Practice 'Conscious Capitalism' Perform 10x Better," *Harvard Business Review*, April 4, 2013.

[4] Adam Morgan, *Eating The Big Fish: How Challenger Brands Can Compete Against Brand Leaders*, (Hoboken, NJ: John Wlley & Sons, 2009); 84.

5

◇◇◇◇◇◇

CUSTOMERS FIRST? NOT SO FAST.

There's a long list of marketing pundits and authors who have made their fortunes selling the idea that putting customers first is the one true path to retail success. Without customers, there is no monetary support for the brand. Without *happy* customers, there's no one to come back and buy whatever it is you're selling, again. And again. And again. What could be more important to a company than building and supporting loyalty among those who patronize the brand? After all, without them, there is no us.

It's easy to see how a company could arrive at that reasoning and completely buy into it. It's misplaced and wrong, but understandable.

A number of years ago, we attended a national retailing conference and had the pleasure of hearing a talk given by Kip Tindell, co-founder and then-CEO of The Container Store. As the leader of a company that's made Fortune Magazine's list of "100 Best Companies to Work For" for a decade and one of the most respected corporate leaders in America, we couldn't wait to hear Tindell's secret to success.

66 | THE VOICE OF THE UNDERDOG

We were not expecting to hear what he said.

To a dumbfounded room of people who were certain they were retailing experts, Tindell said putting customers second had been the key to their company's success. And who were we to argue? At the time, The Container Store had grown at an astounding twenty percent each year since Tindell and his partner opened the first store in 1978.

Instead of customers, Tindell said they made a point to put employees first. He meant it, too. While so many companies identify employees as a "key audience" in their marketing plans, The Container Store is one of the few we know that actually has real strategies for appealing to that audience. In fact, at the time, the company didn't even have a Human Resources department. At The Container Store, HR was a marketing function. "We charge all of our employees with pulling in great talent," Tindell said, adding, "Grade A talent only wants to work with Grade A talent."

Attracting and retaining great talent was the company's highest priority. And Tindell put his money where his mouth was. At that time, The Container Store paid fifty to a hundred percent better than its retail competitors, and offered a 401K plan and medical, dental, and vision plans for both full- and part-time employees. They also invested 241 hours of training per employee against an industry average of just eight. "We're wild-eyed fanatics when it comes to training," Tindell said.

He's also a big believer in communication. In any company, employees have a natural curiosity about where they work and they want to be in the know. They don't want a customer or a friend telling them something they read or heard about their employer.

The only way to build a sense of inclusion is to keep everyone looped in. Tindell and his executive team work to do that constantly. "We have a huge moral obligation to make sure employees look forward to coming to work each morning," he said. At the time of the conference, the company had eleven percent annual employee turnover versus a retail industry average of one hundred percent. Clearly, Tindell was focused on what he considered to be an important personal responsibility.

Why the fanatical focus on employees? Because employees who are positively engaged and challenged deliver excellent customer service. A disengaged, under-compensated, under-trained, unappreciated, and unhappy employee doesn't. It's no more complicated than that.

Look at Chick-fil-A's performance over the past thirty years. Do they have the best chicken sandwich in the business? Most would argue they do. But as good as it is, they didn't vault from a mall food court brand to America's number three QSR brand behind McDonald's and Starbucks based solely on their food. They did it because, year after year, they exponentially outdistance their competitors in customer service. That doesn't happen with unhappy employees who don't feel appreciated or taken care of.

Like Chick-fil-A, The Container Store's goal is to deliver what they call "astonishing customer service." Anyone who has ever visited one of the nearly one hundred Container Stores knows they make good on that promise without exception. Tindell and his leadership team have created an achievement-oriented culture with a balance of challenge and reward, and it is simply more fun to work and perform in an environment like that. Customers spread the word on their good experiences driving more traffic and positive experiences, and the sales and profits ring up.

In 2007, at the time of the conference, Tindell said it's a profit strategy that had driven his company to more than $500 million in sales. In 2019, The Container Store earned revenue just shy of $900 million. Tindell would describe that with two simple words: competitive insulation.

Employees are the ones charged with creating great customer experiences, and when they deliver, they create for their employer a competitive advantage that is extremely difficult to match. Thirty years of positive results is enough to declare The Container Store's strategy a winner.

∞∞∞∞∞

IT'S PERSONAL

While The Container Store and Chick-fil-A are two great examples of how to treat employees the right way, sadly, there are far more examples that illustrate the shadowy side of leadership. Companies don't have souls. But people do. That's never clearer than when company leaders step all over their employees, intentionally or otherwise, turning crushed spirits into crushed brands and broken companies. This experience I had at the gym frames just how quickly that can happen.

As a reformed workout know-it-all, I had engaged the services of a professional trainer to help me sort out my awful form and bad habits. My trainer was a great guy. He was full of passion for a profession he chose as a kid and was excited to be practicing what he preached. Training was clearly his calling, and any fitness chain would have been lucky to have him representing their brand. But this particular day, I could tell something was amiss from the jump. It wasn't anything my trainer said or did. His demeanor was just different. He was less enthusiastic and his trademark energy had been drained. It didn't take a long line of questioning to get to the heart of the matter.

The gym had recently come under new ownership which seemed to be a positive development. They had invested in expensive new equipment, reconditioned the space with fresh paint and carpet, and renamed the place to underscore the forward progress. The capital improvements had been impressive, but the new owners seemed far less concerned with energizing the aspect of the brand that delivers the most important part of the customer experience: the employees.

My friend explained that the gym's new manager had informed all the trainers that they would now be expected to find new clients themselves. Under previous ownership there had been a sales group charged with this task. Now, the trainers were also expected to sell, and they were given aggressive monthly quotas to boot. From the sound of it, the new manager delivered this news to the trainers with all the empathy of Gordon Gekko, Michael Douglas's "greed is good" character from *Wall Street*. To further underscore the urgency of the new requirement, the owners added that the trainers would be fired if they failed. Upon learning this, I was immediately infected with my trainer's dour mood. It was like a contagion. The new owners effectively turned their most effective brand ambassadors into sour brand assassins with a single stupid move.

It's an obvious misstep that may seem like the folly of small-time operators who are in over their heads, but that's not so. Too often, customers are greeted with the vacant stares of disaffected frontline employees performing tasks like zombies nurtured only by their paychecks.

There's a saying that goes, "The fish rots from the head." When a company's culture is built on founder worship—and that founder turns out to be undeserving—the impact on the brand can be devastating. Uber is a prime example.

For his book, *Super Pumped: The Battle for Uber*, New York Times writer Mike Isaac interviewed hundreds of Uber employees who revealed the company's win-at-all-costs culture which led to the downfall of the start-up's CEO, Travis Kalanick. Embroiled in scandals and controversies, Kalanick created a company culture that normalized its founder's bad behavior—everything from drug and alcohol abuse to playboy partying, misogyny, and harassment of both staff and drivers. There was a ranking system for employees, retaliation against those who raised issues or challenged the company culture, and even a federal investigation into allegations of discrimination and unchecked sexual harassment.

Yet, there were those on his staff who idolized him, who "drank the Kool-Aid," if you will, and believed it was Kalanick's drive and ambition that made Uber such a success. In reality, it was his lack of a moral compass that built a toxic culture, and the contagion of abuse led to the unraveling of the brand.

After Kalanick's ousting in 2017, new leadership has tried to recover, but turning such a DNA-ingrained culture is no easy task. It remains to be seen if the company that pioneered the ride-share industry will ultimately win the ride-share game.

Remember Joe Calloway's definition of brand? A brand is what people think it's like to do business with you. Embedded in that important concept is the idea that people do business with other people. And that's not strictly in a face-to-face scenario. You may never see the people at Amazon handling your order, the sourcing, the packing and the shipping, but if they are miserable, what do you think the chances are your fifty-seven packages would have arrived perfectly and on time this year?

If a brand is what people think it's like to do business with you, your employees are the brand. It's great to have a snazzy office and cool things to sell, but the connective energy that flows from strong brands is something only people can generate. How to get that energy flowing is what the next chapter is all about.

6

NEW BEST FRIENDS: WHY HR AND MARKETING SHOULD SHARE AN OFFICE

The most important marketing weapon for a consumer-facing brand isn't advertising. It isn't PR, or social media, or even the products themselves. It's people. In fact, at a time when year by year we do more and more shopping online, how your employees interact with your customers and the brand experience they deliver has never been more critical.

The customer experience is a social one driven by emotion. Whether it's a restaurant, a shoe store, or an airline, the way customers feel about their interactions with the people serving them is the heart of the brand experience. Each exchange either strengthens or weakens the customer's bond with the brand. And what customers think about a company and the way it treats them has the power to make or break that relationship. Great products and smart advertising are potent marketing weapons, but the customer experience trumps everything.

Seems simple enough. Big or small, as the company expands, you hire people, train them up in your way of doing things, and hold them accountable. For decades, companies have spent billions and billions of dollars getting, developing, and implementing bigger, better, longer training. And in large part, it hasn't delivered. Not really. But in the last decade, an alternative to better training has emerged that's as simple as it is revolutionary. It's not easy. But in retrospect, it does seem fairly obvious.

⬦⬦⬦⬦⬦⬦

THE FRIENDLY FOLKS AT CHICK-FIL-A

As we mentioned briefly in the last chapter, Chick-fil-A knows how to deliver a strong customer experience as well as any company. In study after study, Chick-fil-A stands alone as the leader for delivering quality customer service with a gaping chasm separating them from second best. In one study fielded by Coca-Cola, Chick-fil-A's score for friendliness was nearly twice that of the second-friendliest fast food chain, and it scored more than double the category average.

According to the Coke study, friendliness, which is a critical performance indicator in the restaurant category, includes simple pleasantries like saying "please" and "thank you," smiling, and making eye contact. Being polite sounds simple enough. But based on the comparably poor scores for the balance of the fast-food chains in the study, it's exceedingly difficult to get front-line employees to extend themselves. The question is, why? What's so tough about smiling and saying "thank you?"

The reality is unfortunate for most companies, because it couldn't be more important. As social beings, we're constantly evaluating our daily experiences based on social interaction and feedback. An evaluative loop whirls away in our minds behind the scenes giving us constant information about our sense of belonging, status, self-respect, and so forth. In fact, this process is so fundamental to our human experience, we tend to forget about it.

Too often, as marketers, we do forget about it, or at the very least, we overlook it. But not at Chick-fil-A. From leadership to the front line, they always remember that delivering quality social experiences is core to their success. And that begs the question: In a society where the prevailing consensus is that basic civility and good manners are on the decline, how does a company train people to be well-mannered and friendly? How do we teach employees to show up socially in a manner that invites people to connect with our brand? The answer is, you don't.

You hire them.

Chick-fil-A founder Truett Cathy addressed this very question directly in a 2005 interview. In it, he acknowledged the tremendous energy the company puts into training and retaining employees, but he said the key is to begin the process by selecting the right people in the first place. Not surprisingly, Chick-fil-A is extraordinarily selective when hiring. Instead of trying to train people to say "please" and "thank you," Chick-fil-A hires people who already say "please" and "thank you." Cathy summed it up in the interview saying, "We give them good training, but I expect them to bring their personalities with them."

It's tempting to dismiss the company's commitment to careful hiring as the byproduct of some unseen advantage. But Chick-fil-A enjoys no such thing. The company slugs it out in the wildly competitive fast-food restaurant segment against industry titans with huge marketing war chests like McDonald's, Burger King, Wendy's, Subway, Dunkin' Donuts, and hordes of others. To make matters even more challenging, capacity in the fast-food segment has been outstripping population growth for nearly two decades. And the front-line jobs at these restaurants aren't high paying or particularly fun, compounding the recruiting challenge.

Anybody who has worked in a restaurant environment can attest to the long hours, fast pace, and just plain hard work. The company's commitment to finding people who work hard with smiles on their faces boils down to just that: commitment. Chick-fil-A leadership believes in the difference people make, and they focus on recruitment and retention through practices that consistently deliver the best front-line employees in the industry. The company's enviable financials underscore the efficacy of the approach. In 2017, in just over 2,200 locations in forty-seven states and Washington, D.C, Chick-fil-A reported more than $9 billion in revenue, marking fifty years of sales growth. That's more than $4 million a year per store in a fast food restaurant that's only open six days a week.

⚬⚬⚬⚬⚬⚬

MAKE NO MISTAKE—CHICK-FIL-A ISN'T A UNICORN

"Anybody who doesn't understand that companies are in business to make a profit isn't plugged in right."

That colorful sentiment was issued by a colleague to drive home his point that delivering great customer service isn't an end unto itself. In far-reaching research for his book *Firms of Endearment*, Dr. Raj Sisodia discovered that companies holding excellent customer service as one of their core tenets returned an average of 1,111% over a ten year period as compared with 122% for the S&P 500 over the same period. "What's most significant about this is that we didn't set out to find companies that outperform the stock market," Sisodia said in a 2009 presentation. Sisodia was looking for examples of companies driven by passion and purpose when he found the corresponding impressive financial performances that also tied back to a relentless focus on the customer experience.

The list of companies he identifies in the book as standouts include Amazon, BMW, CarMax, Commerce Bank, Costco, eBay, Harley-Davidson, Honda, IKEA, JetBlue, L.L.Bean, Patagonia, REI, Southwest Airlines, Starbucks, The Container Store, Trader Joe's, UPS, Wegmans Food Markets, and Whole Foods. The practices Sisodia says these companies employ to ensure great customer experiences include the following:

- Hiring people with a passion for their work resulting in better employee retention
- Paying relatively modest executive salaries, but giving rank-and-file employees more in salaries and benefits than comparable companies
- Cultivating a culture of openness from the top down
- Devoting time to training and developing employees
- Empowering employees at all levels to make on-the-spot

decisions to ensure customer satisfaction
- Creating close relationships with customers
- Viewing corporate culture as a great business asset

The truth is, until a company is delivering an optimal customer experience through excellent and consistent customer service, it isn't well positioned to achieve maximum benefit from advertising or any other marketing activity.

The marketing process should begin and end with the customer experience. Service perfection is not a realistic goal, of course, and even the most committed companies find it difficult to achieve and maintain high standards consistently. (Even Chick-fil-A tops out around an eighty-seven in the annual American Customer Satisfaction Index.) Service excellence requires a shared commitment among leadership, sustained institutional attention, and deliberate practice over time. But it's a critical starting point for the entire marketing planning process.

The best advertising leverages something inherently true and valuable about a brand and delivers it to current and new customers in a compelling way. Advertising invites people to experience the brand and makes an implicit promise to deliver what it's selling. If that promise is broken by a surly, inattentive, or otherwise disengaged employee, more harm than good is done to the brand. When the customer's experience of the brand—his or her impression of what it's like to do business with the company— fails to meet the expectation set by the advertising, it creates a disconnect. That disconnect is often irreparable, and in some circumstances, it has the power to create a passionately disaffected customer, otherwise known as a "brand terrorist." Research on word-of-mouth communication suggests people are ten times more likely to talk about a negative experience than a positive one.[1] And social media makes it easy to share that misery with the world.

Great customer experiences have the opposite effect. An army of wildly satisfied customers can function as brand ambassadors or "evangelists" and dramatically reduce the need to advertise in the traditional sense. Starbucks, Harley-Davidson, and The Container Store are just a few of the companies that rely almost exclusively on positive customer experiences to do the bulk of their advertising for them. And while Chick-fil-A is a heavy advertiser, the company's high customer service level allows it to steer clear of promoting product discounts, a margin-erasing tactic that drives the rest of the industry. Instead, Chick-fil-A uses its advertising dollars to build and reinforce its already formidable brand and to create further identity distinction in a category consumed by parity. As a result, its legions of loyal followers are the envy of the industry as are the revenue and profits the brand generates per location.

⬦⬦⬦⬦⬦⬦

WHY MARKETING'S NEW POWER COUPLE REALLY IS A GAME CHANGER

If it's not obvious already, for challenger brands of all shapes and sizes, hiring the right people is the fuel that will drive your brand forward. Finding, training, and keeping people who are enthusiastic about delivering your brand experience is the point of leverage against larger rivals.

In a *Harvard Business Review* blog post I've kept for years, *Fast Company* co-founder Bill Taylor suggested that HR and marketing must conspire to create truly great brand experiences. Taylor said, "The new 'power couple' inside the best companies, I concluded, was an iron-clad partnership between marketing leadership and HR leadership. Your brand is your culture, your culture is your brand."[2]

The good news for challenger brands is that people are often a huge problem for market leaders. While size and scale are advantages for driving efficiency and market leverage, it works against the people side of the business where authentic emotional connections are required to drive strong corporate culture. Personal connections don't scale very well, which is why the corporate cultures of the world's largest organizations aren't often held up as examples for the rest. A quick peek at any year's "Fortune 100 Best Companies to Work For" list underscores the point.

A quick story about the difference the right (and wrong) people can make. As we've noted more than a few times, The Container Store is legendary for its employee-focused culture, and as such, the company has been on Fortune's coveted list many times. When founder Kip Tindell put the company up for sale in 2008, Best Buy was among more than one hundred suitors that expressed serious interest. Best Buy leadership admired The Container Store's culture and hoped to imbue its own with The Container Store's special esprit de corps through acquisition. But Tindell knew better and wouldn't entertain the offer. He understood that culture can't be purchased. It has to be created and cultivated organically. And this is something that leaders in smaller companies often do well, because they're closer to the action. They're in touch. Challengers can use the advantage of smaller size to out-hire, out-train, and out-retain bigger rivals. The result can be a brand experience that's impossible to duplicate regardless of resources. Finding, training and keeping people who are enthusiastic about delivering your brand experience is the point of leverage against larger rivals.

◇◇◇◇◇◇

FOOTNOTES

1 Andrew Thomas, "The Secret Ratio That Proves Why Customer Reviews Are So Important," *Inc.* Feb. 26, 2018.

2 Bill Taylor, "Brand Is Culture, Culture Is Brand," *Harvard Business Review*, Sept. 27, 2010.

7

✕✕✕✕✕✕

IT'S WHAT CHALLENGERS SAY, THEN DO

Trusted Brands Win Hearts

We all know people who say one thing and do another. It's not a very attractive quality. Most of us get this wrong once in a while, but some people clearly take the promises behind their word far more seriously than others. People who routinely deliver on their promises are generally held in high regard and with very good reason. Consistent behavior is predictable and that which can be predicted can be trusted. Trust serves as the foundational component for creating anything of substance and durability. Nothing much good is possible in its absence, and boundless possibility blossoms in its presence.

Our emotions are finely tuned for reading signals that tell us whether or not someone or something can be counted on to perform as expected. It's an intuition gifted to each of us at birth and honed and sharpened through an unyielding flow of lifetime experiences that either deliver or fail to deliver as anticipated. Knowing who to trust, what to trust, and when to trust is essential for our survival. So critical is our ability to discern with reliable accuracy that it extends to every relationship we have and every decision we make. Trust is the essential bonding agent for relationships of any sort, and our relationships with brands are no exception.

The thing we look for most of all when we're assessing trust is congruence, or the agreement between what is said and what is done. We like people who walk their talk and do it with predictable consistency. Our expectations are met when a person's values and behavior square up. When people live according to their values, psychologists say they have personal congruence, and we say they have integrity. When people behave in congruent ways, we can better understand them. This, too, is true for our relationships with brands.

People are generally attracted to those who reflect their own values, which is the truism behind the expression, "Birds of a feather flock together." Much of the human psychology that undergirds our interpersonal relationships extends to our relationships with brands and our efforts to market them. In fact, our innate desire for associating with people like us is the organizing principle behind all of marketing. Nothing much could be accomplished in the world of marketing and advertising if people weren't drawn to others who look, act, and think as they do. Everything marketers do is aimed at drawing a crowd for their brand, and doing that well requires them to stay focused on its values, signal them clearly, and then actually behave in ways that are consistent with those values. When brands are aligned this way, we say they are congruent. The stronger a brand's congruence, the more attractive it becomes.

When a brand is congruent around things we value, it has what it needs to become important to us. In this sense, a brand's personality functions no differently than our own. When brands get this absolutely right, they take on a very special quality that the team at Eat Big Fish describes as a "Lighthouse Identity." Lighthouse brands broadcast their personalities so strongly that consumers take notice whether they're looking for them or not. They're the brands we can't ignore. Famous brands like Dove, Southwest Airlines, Disney, Target, Mini Cooper, Patagonia, and scores more like them make routine appearances on lists of most likeable brands because the people behind those brands are radically committed to curating and expressing their brand's congruence. They're the best-in-class brands whose congruence gives off beacon-like clarity that glows in the dark, and their brilliance helps us find our way through crowded and confusing consumer categories. They're the category benchmarks.

Most Lighthouse brands are not top dogs in their respective categories, but their bark is unmistakable. Market leaders struggle against challenger brands for reasons that can be traced to the unique advantages afforded by the underdog's smaller scale. Challenger brands can act more nimbly than market leaders, which often releases them from the binds of category conventions that restrict the top dogs. Beyond breaking with tradition, the cleverest challengers find ways to turn their limitations into significant advantages. Challenger brands can make and keep commitments with their customers in ways market leaders often can't or simply won't, and, in doing so, can create enviable affinity for themselves. What's more, challengers can often focus in ways that market leaders find difficult, often giving birth to surprising new segments. It's this capacity for brand focus and cultural alignment around a single-minded mission that has served as the catalyst for countless challenger brand successes.

◇◇◇◇◇◇

FOCUS FOSTERS TRUST

In the crowded '90s-era soft drink category dominated by Coke and Pepsi, tiny Red Bull showed up in the U.S. with a relentlessly aggressive grassroots focus on extreme sports and singlehandedly created the energy drink segment it would soon dominate. Red Bull flipped category convention on its head with a single oddly-packaged, premium-priced, eight-ounce can of rocket fuel with the simple promise that it would give you wings. The claim that its ingredients actually fueled athletic performance was in doubt from the jump, but that was not the point at all. Red Bull did something even more important for its carefully selected audience than give them a buzz. It embraced with unapologetic enthusiasm their belief that limits are for losers.

When adrenaline junkies met Red Bull, they didn't see a beverage company. They saw a kindred spirit. No start-up beverage company could afford to go toe-to-toe with the category killers through traditional advertising channels, and Red Bull was no different. So they turned that limitation into their advantage.

Red Bull had no choice but to make it personal, so they met their customers where they were—at local extreme sports events and competitions. But they didn't just send in product reps wearing logoed shirts. They sent enthusiasts and greeted local fans with people who looked and behaved just like them. They got involved and organized events, handing out free samples of their product and offering modest sponsorships to the minor extreme sports celebrities who held sway. Red Bull's early hands-on efforts succeeded in something few brands try to do.

Remarkably, Red Bull succeeded by recognizing and then building the social context for the role the brand would assume. Through intense engagement and aggressive support of extreme sport athletes and fans alike, Red Bull built its reputation as *their* champion. The company ushered in a new era of influencer marketing whose magic is its execution by peers for peers. In doing so, Red Bull built and fortified an unassailable brand advantage the cola giants never saw coming.

By virtue of its strong brand congruence and the behavior it informs, Red Bull has become a trusted and influential extreme sports industry insider. It has become a brand for the fans, catalyzing the community with extraordinary engagement and nourishing the very ecosystem that supports it. They've done this not by showing up and selling product, but by offering real value to the extreme sports community. And while doing all of that, Red Bull did something else that would make it the envy of its peers; Red Bull transformed into a media company capitalizing on its authentic credibility. Who better to carry the message of the extreme sports junkie than the sport's number one ambassador and keeper of the flame?

A quick review of redbull.com today reveals its enviable role as the center pole propping up the tent for extreme sports enthusiasts around the globe. Red Bull has done the best job of thinking about their brand like journalists, and they stay busy at work in their very own newsroom cranking out content they know their audience will love. The key to Red Bull's success has been its airtight alignment between what it promised customers and the way it behaves while delivering on that promise. Red Bull didn't simply target its users. It assumed its place among them. With $7 billion in 2019 sales, Red Bull enjoys a Lighthouse Identity in a category it created as a challenger and ranks third on the U.S. soft drink category leaderboard.

There's no escaping the attention of competitors with that kind of success, and Red Bull now has company in the category it created, but not from Coke or Pepsi. As so often is the case, it seems that the many penalties of size have served to constrict an adequate response from the cola giants, leaving room for another inspired challenger.

Soon after Red Bull demonstrated that some consumers were willing to pay 300% more for 33% less product, another cagey challenger brand made its appearance. Monster Energy joined Red Bull's party and quickly identified more open ground. No brand can cover all the territory, so it stood to reason another competitor would find a foothold in the energy drink segment. While Red Bull focused on extreme sports, Monster dug deeper still and isolated its attention on the original extreme sport—motorsports, and motorcycle racing in particular. Here again, it was Monster's relentless focus on an under-appreciated niche paired with its masterful cultivation of its own brand congruence that won fans and launched the brand to unexpected heights.

Unless you're a motorsports fan, Monster's success is likely to hit you as something of a mystery because, like Red Bull, the company didn't rely on advertising to achieve it. Instead, Monster turned all of its early marketing resources toward the goal of courting fans of Supercross, an indoor dirt bike racing series held in stadiums around the country. Taking a page out of Red Bull's playbook, Monster adopted Supercross fans as their own and went to work creating genuine value for them by reimagining and then recreating the fan experience. Monster connected deeply with Supercross by behaving like fans—something that furthered their insight into the customers the brand was trying to attract. Rather than focusing on selling product, the company sought to boost the entertainment value of Supercross events and help grow the sport. Monster accomplished both of those goals and used the experience to expand into more prestigious racing formats.

In 2017, Monster became a title sponsor for NASCAR: The Monster Energy NASCAR Cup Series. Over the past twenty years, and pretty much under the radar, Monster grew sales north of $3 billion. In the process, it became the best performing stock in the U.S. for fifteen consecutive years, with share growth of 60,000%.[1] From out of nowhere, Monster became a status brand for motorsports fans across all formats. That's an extraordinary accomplishment for a company selling cans of highly priced carbonated sugar water. Consumer allegiance like this is available to any challenger brand if they understand how to behave like category insiders.

START WITH CULTURE

Red Bull and Monster accomplished something every brand wants and carved out a marketplace position that can't be co-opted by the competition. Not even mighty Coca-Cola has succeeded in disturbing the trajectory of these high-flying challengers. Not that it isn't trying.

In 2019, the company rolled out its first energy drink under the Coke brand. Coke Energy hit the shelves in the United Kingdom touting its ingredients with a hopelessly predictable invitation to "try a new and different energy drink that is designed to complement upbeat and busy lives."[2] Anytime the category killer flexes its muscle, competitors are well advised to pay attention, but the odds of Red Bull or Monster-like success for Coke's uninspired offering are long indeed. That's because it's the behavior of the brand that defines the challenger, and, as we've already seen, it's a company's culture that drives the brand's behavior. Any hope for the kind of brand congruence that drives definitive brand distinction rests on the successful alignment of brand values and cultural values. Get this wrong and there's little hope for high brand performance. Get it right, and the resulting congruence will separate a brand from the crowd.

In this sense, culture serves as the fundamental challenger brand advantage. Best of all, a big advertising budget isn't required for achieving this advantage. All that's required is commitment, but not ordinary commitment. Challenger brand cultures are shaped by the passion of their people for the values they all share and the purpose that defines them. They're relentlessly focused on only the things that matter for living out their brand values. It's a level of commitment that's only possible when a brand's values are tightly aligned with the personal values of the people responsible for it.

As consumers, we recognize this when we see it because it's not our usual experience. We want more of it, and we reward it. It's the authentic friendliness we're greeted with at Chick-fil-A, the enthusiasm we might share with an Apple Store employee for our favorite gadget, or the kindred foodie spirit we encounter at Whole Foods. It's always about the human connection consumers make with the brands they love.

While this is obvious for service sector companies, it's also true for manufacturing-based brands. The most successful products connect on an emotional level and take on significance well beyond their utility value. The best customer experiences happen when products and services are supported by employees who share the brand's values, believe in the company's purpose, and show up as enthusiastic enlistees in the company's mission. It's a tall order to be sure, but companies that benefit from deep alignment between brand and culture radiate their distinction from the inside out. And in doing so, they make it difficult for customers to ignore them and impossible for competitors to encroach.

Brand congruence like this can only be achieved when leaders are themselves congruent with their brand. That's because leaders set the pace for culture. As we've seen in previous chapters, leadership sets the tone for the way a company behaves. The magic unleashed when culture matches brand is the unlocking move for challengers. Brand congruence energizes organizational behavior, clarifies priorities and decision-making, brings necessary focus to the mission, and creates and fortifies true brand distinction. Most importantly, challengers that benefit from strong brand congruence attract the right people to their cause in what often looks to outsiders like a conspiracy for success. Of course, this doesn't happen by accident. It starts inside at the very top with vision and clarity of purpose.

⬥⬥⬥⬥⬥⬥⬥

BRANDING FROM THE INSIDE OUT

In 1992, a young Stefan Pierer paid $4 million to buy KTM Motorcycles from its creditors with an eye on a quick turnaround. It was regarded by many as a sucker's bet. Once an Austrian icon, the brand's luster had faded in lock step with its loss of industry respect. Worse yet, the brand had become a target of derision for customers who'd been burned by bad bikes while the company slowly collapsed under the weight of poor stewardship. It's one thing to start from scratch with a clean slate as an unknown brand and quite another to carry the burden of a bad reputation.

KTM had become the butt of jokes, if it was a topic at all, and when the jokes were no longer funny, the brand was all but forgotten. Such are the hazards of a fickle market that cycles quickly on the steady churn of fresh young buyers with short attention spans and a taste for the next new model. If the brand's health worked against Pierer, the state of the motorcycle market offered no help whatsoever. The market for motorcycles was shrinking in the '90s, and fury had turned to frenzy among a group of aggressive rivals who offered high quality products and value KTM couldn't match.

With its claim to half the motorcycle market, Honda (with a gaggle of Japanese challengers in tow) held firm ground right where KTM needed to rebuild. None of the news was good. As he considered options for his brand, Pierer surveyed a market in decline filled with cutthroat competitors cast against a cynical industry and a wake of jaded consumers. Add to this mash-up of misery a dealer network that had been all but dismantled by the company's demise. Nobody wanted Pierer's motorcycles, which was painfully apparent to the dealers who sold them. With no customers and slim prospects, Pierer made a bold decision that would prove to be pivotal for the future of his brand. It was a choice wholly informed by the challenger ethos, and it would ultimately serve to catapult the brand into an enviable and unassailable premium position, win the hearts of enthusiasts worldwide, and send KTM past Harley-Davidson as the leading motorcycle maker outside of Asia.[3] Pierer's decision? He went racing.

In 1993, just a year after buying KTM, Pierer assigned a full quarter of his annual operating budget to the task of winning the famous Paris to Dakar Rally, an unforgiving three-week race across the Sahara. KTM's first try at the Dakar was met with equal parts astonishment and amusement by industry observers and certainly no immediate success. But it sent a message about the destiny Pierer had envisioned for the brand.

Moves like this often make little sense from the outside looking in, but the decision to go racing signaled something important from the inside out about the behavior Pierer wanted at KTM. It told those in its employ and those who would one day be, exactly what was expected for the brand and of the people who controlled its destiny. The company's relentless focus on racing laid the bedrock for a budding culture that would be driven by performance and serve to define the character of KTM. Of course, focus offered no immediate fix. Early racing efforts met with failure, and there was no overnight success. The company struggled for the better part of a decade with all the challenges of a brand in distress, but the company culture was growing stronger and more committed to its cause. Eight years and eight successive tries later, KTM claimed victory at Dakar, besting stalwart brands and winning legions of new fans.

In 2001, the company's relentless focus on its singular purpose paid off, and with the determination of a relentless champion, it has paid off again and again every year since, earning KTM eighteen consecutive Dakar victories and building a reputation as the brand that wins. The importance of Pierer's decision to shape the brand's trajectory and its ultimate success is impossible to overstate. The company's single-minded focus helped create the sort of brand congruence challengers can use to claim and fortify formidable advantage. KTM built its brand position from the inside out by focusing first on creating a culture that the industry's most influential customers would love.

What Pierer understood from the start is that racing sets the pace in the motorcycle industry. From professional athletes to hometown racetrack heroes, competition shapes the industry narrative about its brands and race fans know the score. They're the influencers of the industry and KTM created an appeal especially for them with the kind of clarity of purpose they hadn't seen from a motorcycle manufacturer before.

Winning the hearts and minds of motorcycle racers informs the ethos at KTM. Every decision its leaders make is advised by the company's mantra-like brand tagline, "Ready to Race," which serves double duty as its own internal cultural call to action. KTM's cultural commitment to racing has driven everything from the types of motorcycles they build to the people they employ right down to the retail dealer network they've developed. Unlike competitors who sold machines through multi-line dealers, KTM required single-line commitment from its dealers who themselves were racers. It's a strategy that continues to pay dividends. The manufacturer is on pace to double output by the end of 2020, while the balance of the two-wheeler market declines by fifteen percent.[4]

The KTM brand has been formed in every respect by its culture in what has become a virtuous loop of self-reinforcing behavior that matches precisely the messages it sends to consumers. The synergy between KTM's culture, brand, advertising, and experience at retail gives off the attractive clarity of a Lighthouse Identity. KTM promised it would be for racers, and it delivered. KTM built trust through its behavior among a core audience of influencers, and that reverberated among consumers.

When brands enjoy high levels of congruence, they set and meet high customer expectations, and in so doing, build the essential trust of customers. When they do this very well, they can even occupy a singular position in their category for which there is no suitable replacement. Brands like Red Bull, Monster, and KTM achieve their ends by first clarifying who they are and who they're for, and then by building their brands from the inside out—beginning with company culture.

⋄⋄⋄⋄⋄⋄⋄

FOOTNOTES

[1] Theron, Mohamed, "This century's best-performing US stock sells energy drinks, not iPhones," *Business Insider*, April 16, 2019.

[2] Simon Gwynn, "Coca-Cola takes on Red Bull with Coke-branded energy drink," *Campaign*, Mar. 28, 2019.

[3] Richard Weiss, "Motorcycle Maker KTM Passes Harley and Aims at Kawasaki," *Bloomberg Businessweek*, June 11, 2019.

[4] Ketan Thakkar and Nehal Chaliawala, "KTM Attracting New Buyers, Keen to Double Volumes in Two Years," *The Economic Times*, Sept. 24, 2019.

8

<><><><><><>

START AT THE TOP

*Why Culture Has to be Embraced
and Championed by Leadership*

When you look out over the vast panoply of American companies, both old and new, there is no shortage of iconic "out front" leaders with whom those companies are identified. While many like Bill Gates (Microsoft), Phil Knight (Nike), Richard Branson (Virgin), and Jeff Bezos (Amazon) started their companies from scratch and still have a strong hand in leading them, others like Lee Iacocca (Chrysler), Roger Enrico (Pepsi), and Bob Iger (Disney) entered their leadership roles at key inflection points in the revivals of their companies, serving as highly visible stewards of their respective brands for a limited time. A few, like Steve Jobs, had the fascinating distinction of checking both of those boxes.

On another level of branding identity, America also has a rich history of corporations like Ford, Eddie Bauer, Ben & Jerry's, Trump, and Neiman Marcus that took on the name and personality of their founders both literally and figuratively. Not surprisingly, when the company namesakes were intimately involved in leadership from the founding forward, the brand personality and company culture tended to mirror the founder and stay fairly consistent, for better or worse. In some companies, that led to stagnant and myopic leadership. In others, it kept the course of the corporate ship steady through the turbulent waters of the 20th and now 21st centuries.

Clearly, there are many kinds of leaders and an equal number of leadership situations you may find yourself navigating. But through it all, one thing remains constant in the cases of the most successful leaders, and that's the crucial role of culture. Whether you're a founder, or a temporary steward of leadership, if you're the head of your company, or even a key leader in the management team, you have an obligation and a responsibility to own the culture in your company. If it's positive, you can fully embrace and shepherd the culture you find, or in the case of a toxic culture, take the responsibility for changing it. But what you cannot do under any circumstances is ignore it.

∞∞∞∞∞

WELCOME TO THE MATRIX

Admittedly, the concept of company culture may feel like a vague, amorphous, unquantifiable thing that's impossible to get your arms around. And that would be fair. In many ways, culture is like the air we breathe. We don't always see it and, often, we can't feel it. But in ways we can't perceive until we physically feel its effects, culture can inspire us and fill us with the energy and heart to reach beyond our wildest limitations. It can also turn toxic and kill us on the spot.

If you're a sci-fi fan, there's a better than even chance that the last weekend of March, 1999, you were in a movie theatre watching a mind-blowing new film called *The Matrix*. Written and directed by Lana and Lilly Wachowski, *The Matrix* tells the story of a dystopian future where humanity is trapped inside a simulated reality. In a now classic scene toward the beginning of the film, Morpheus (played by Laurence Fishburne), the leader of the rebellion against the machines, offers computer hacker and future savior Neo (played by Keanu Reeves) the chance to know or ignore the truth about The Matrix by swallowing either a red or a blue pill.

"Do you want to know what it is?" Morpheus asks, referring to The Matrix. When Neo nods, Morpheus continues. "The Matrix is everywhere. It is all around us. Even now in this very room. You can see it when you look out the window, or when you turn on your television. You can feel it when you go to work, when you go to church, when you pay your taxes. Unfortunately, no one can be told what The Matrix is. You have to see it for yourself."

The dystopian AI aside, company culture is very much like The Matrix. It's everywhere we are, it affects everything we do, and it's something from which we cannot be separated. When companies have no discernable culture to speak of, employees will note the lack of it and privately sense how much they wish their company had one. But when cultures are strong, people who work in them will describe the culture as palpable. I ran headfirst into one of those the day I started my first job in Dallas.

In 1992, Tracy Locke had come to Atlanta to recruit creatives from Portfolio Center, and I was fortunate to receive one of the offers they made. As it turned out, Pepsi-Cola was the first and only account I'd work on for my first eighteen months at the agency, and the brand couldn't have been further from my consciousness or heart. Coming from Atlanta, Coca-Cola wasn't a choice. It was part of who you were as a southerner and, in my case, I had spent the previous decade nursing a constant drip of Diet Coke. I bought it cases at a time and had never even dreamed of drinking anything else.

On my first day at the agency, one of the group creative directors took the other newbies and me on an agency tour and at some point, I asked what I thought was a fairly ubiquitous question, "Where is the Coke machine?" Immediately, the person leading the tour stopped in her tracks, wheeled around and stared me in the eye. "We don't have Coke machines here," she said. "There's a Pepsi machine on each floor in the break rooms." It was as if I had insulted her children. A few days later as I was recounting the story to one of the senior art directors I was working with and remarking on how over the top my tour guide had been, he laughed that Pepsi was now all he drank both at the office and at home. "Not me,"' I countered. "I'll drink Diet Pepsi here if I have to, but at home, I'm still drinking Diet Coke." With the straightest face possible, looking almost a little hurt, he said, "Really?" I said, "What? I'm one guy. Me drinking Diet Pepsi isn't going to make the slightest bit of difference to PepsiCo's sales." His reply? "Yeah, but what if everyone thought that way?"

I didn't drink another Diet Coke for almost two years.

Cultural cultivation starts at the top. Before you can expect those who work for you to not only lean into your culture, but to become stewards and protectors of it, you have to own it yourself and go all in. The adventurous spirit of Virgin flows directly from Richard Branson through everyone who works for him. At Pixar, the creative, collaborative spirit established by John Lasseter and Ed Catmull is the life force that drives visionaries like Pete Docter, Andrew Stanton, Brad Bird, and the rest of the team to make blockbuster after blockbuster. At Zappos, the obsession with exemplary customer service starts with CEO Tony Hsieh, but that's hardly where it stops.

The best company cultures aren't projects. They aren't "management initiatives" or "this year's focus to improve morale." Your culture is as much of who you are as the products and services you sell, or the people who sell them. And when you get it right, the effects echo for centuries.

Henry Ford's commitment to innovation is still alive and kicking 116 years after the founding of Ford Motor Company. Truett Cathy's vision for Chick-fil-A's customer service model has lasted for seventy-three years and only shows signs of getting stronger as CFA is now the third largest restaurant chain in America. Herb Kelleher's dream to democratize the skies with Southwest Airlines famously started with a three-route triangle sketch on a cocktail napkin in 1971. Today, Southwest's fun, infectious culture of customer love is stronger than ever and delivered daily by nearly sixty thousand employees from HR and management to the flight crews and the branding team.

Great cultures don't happen by accident. They're intentional. And if you're a leader of an agency, or a company, or a brand, or any other enterprise where people are working to realize a vision, it's incumbent that you take the reins as the author of your culture.

That's not to say you have to do everything it takes to establish a culture—or change one that already exists—all by yourself. That's an impossible task. But make no mistake, your team keys off of your mindset and your behavior when it comes to making sense of what your company stands for. They will assign importance to the things you pay attention to and they will embrace what they see you embrace. Your first step toward building a spectacular culture is deciding what those things should be.

◇◇◇◇◇◇◇

INTENTIONALLY BUILD THE CULTURE YOU WANT

No culture can exist, much less thrive, that is incongruent with the fundamental purpose and values at the core of your company. Culture, purpose, and values work together, and at their greatest realization, your culture reflects your purpose and values fully manifested in every person who works for you. As the leader of your brand, it's incumbent on you to establish that purpose. To define those values. And to be your company's North Star when it comes to living into them.

Take another look at Zappos, the online shoe and clothing company. You could search the world and you won't find a company more obsessed with culture and values and the role they play in the company's success. At Zappos, culture and values aren't just well-meaning aspirations buried in an employee handbook. From very early on, CEO Tony Hsieh laid out the ten core values his company stood for and then created an intentional HR hiring gauntlet defined by those values that every new employee has had to run through in order to get a job.

It's not that Zappos' values are incredibly complicated, or difficult to understand:

- Deliver WOW through service
- Embrace and drive change
- Create fun and a little weirdness
- Be adventurous, creative, and open-minded
- Pursue growth and learning
- Build open and honest relationships with communication
- Build a positive team and family spirit
- Do more with less
- Be passionate and determined
- Be humble[1]

The magic lies in the commitment the company has made to making sure each employee embraces and lives into each value in everything they do on the company's behalf. How do they do that? For starters, they hire slowly to make sure each hire is the right one. Cultural fit is the first step of the Zappos hiring process, accounting for fifty percent of the person's value. Fail that step and you're out before ever talking to the hiring manager.

Once hired, each person is fully trained against each of the company's core values. They spend the first three to four weeks in the call center learning how to provide exemplary customer service and at the end of that time, each person is offered $2,000 to leave the company. Each successive year for the next three years, the "price to quit" goes up by $1,000. Think about that. Zappos would rather pay someone $5,000 to go away than have an employee who isn't fully bought into its brand culture and its values.

How many people do you have in your organization right now who aren't fully engaged with your purpose, your values, or your culture?

At LOOMIS, we've spent the last twenty years living into our culture, and it hasn't always been easy. Winning new accounts and having to hire quickly to accommodate the new work has often put us to the test. Having to make difficult staffing decisions when we found ourselves in a place of contraction tested our values even more. Growing from fifteen to sixty-five employees was a blessing, but it also challenged our ability to maintain quality and consistency.

Acquiring companies with their own cultures. Merging in others. They all presented challenges to maintaining our culture and most of all, doing the right thing even when it was hard. Like Zappos, our core values aren't particularly difficult or complex. But where the rubber meets the road, they've definitely been tested. Here's an honest look at what some of that has looked like.

SHARED SUCCESS—Where We Go One, We Go All

Over our history, we've had a lot of success with new business wins, and when it was possible to share a windfall at the end of the year, we did. When there were agency perks to be had, they were enjoyed by all. There wasn't one set of benefits for the leaders and a second set for everyone else. We were in this together, through good and bad. When looming deadlines and an impossible workload threatened late nights at the office, we stepped in and helped. Our feeling has always been it's better for many to stay until eight than one person to stay until midnight.

For more than twenty years now, we've looked out for each other and, collectively, won more than our fair share of business. But like every agency, we've also had clients who left. Sometimes, big clients that weren't easy to replace quickly. On more than one occasion, rather than sending people out the door, we chose temporary pay cuts. Everyone took them, with principals taking the first and largest percentage cuts, management second and lower by percentage, and so on by position from the top down. When the sun came up again, salaries were restored in reverse order.

It sucked, plain and simple. But we got through it together and with a renewed sense of familial unity. We endured the battle together and came out stronger on the other side.

FAMILY & FRIENDSHIP—The Golden Rule Is the Most Important Rule

There's a reason every religious text in the world includes a version of The Golden Rule. It's the same reason "love the other person more than you love yourself" is the prescription for a happy marriage. Ask the more than three hundred people who have ever worked at LOOMIS for a description, and more often than not, the word you'll get back is "family." That may sound a bit cliché, but when you're in the middle of the fight, it certainly doesn't feel that way. Like every family, we don't always agree on everything. But through years of intentional work, we've made our default position one of love, caring, thoughtfulness, and friendship. We listen first and always try to treat our clients, our partners, our vendors, and each other how we would also like to be treated.

HIGH PERFORMANCE—The Harder We Work, the Luckier We Get

If there's anything our team at LOOMIS prides itself on, it's our extraordinary work ethic. It has been that way since the day we opened the doors, and we can honestly say it has never been any other way. From the beginning, we knew no one was ever going to give us anything, and we've fought the fight accordingly. Looking back, you can see that mindset reflected in our original mission statement: "You can outspend us, but you'll rarely outthink us, and you'll never outwork us."

Hard work is one of the key core values to the agency's culture and success, and as much as we love the idea of magic, we haven't yet found anything that replaces rolling up your sleeves and gutting it out. Going the extra mile to achieve greatness is the mettle we look for in every person we hire. It's also how we know when we get it wrong. When you work with a pack of overachievers, there's no place to hide if that's not your thing. We set the bar high and get after it day after day. Over the years, when we made a wrong hire, it was apparent in a matter of days. And in almost every case, we'd moved too quickly and failed to do our due diligence in making sure that person was a great cultural fit. I'm betting Zappos has very few hires they look back on with regret.

INTEGRITY—Do the Right Thing, Even When Nobody's Looking

More than any of our other core values, maintaining integrity is the most expected and, frankly, the most cliché. It's also the value that's most fundamental and most non-negotiable for your team and especially those in leadership. If your people can't trust that you will do the right thing even when it's hard, when you're unchallenged, or when nobody's looking, they'll never fully buy into the direction you set and the leadership you offer. On the contrary, if the people you lead physically see you make the hard decisions, turn down unethical requests, fight for their well-being against unfair demands, and personally experience your authentic, unwavering commitment to honesty and integrity, they'll line up to follow you into hell. We've seen it happen.

Within a year of the agency starting—when we were in real need of revenue—a potential client offered to give us a nice piece of business. All he wanted in return was for us to buy him a souped-up Mac laptop. For some, a lucrative piece of business for a computer might seem like a no-brainer. It was for us, too. We turned down the account and never looked back. Integrity doesn't work on a sliding scale. Right is right, no matter what. Twenty years later, we were approached by another client that would have added millions to our annual revenue. There was nothing untoward about it, but it didn't fit well with the values of the agency. And while many would have been excited to work on the account, it would have caused heartache and turmoil for others. We politely declined that account as well.

We have always felt a sincere responsibility both for our employees and their families, and that can add pressure to decisions with financial ramifications. What's crystal clear is that your culture and your values have to be non-negotiable. At some point as a leader, you will most likely find yourself faced with the unenviable choice between your values and a financial windfall. Choosing integrity may feel expensive, but in truth, it's invaluable.

GROWTH & IMPROVEMENT—There Is No Finish Line

There's a saying in both business and self-improvement that "if you're not moving forward, you're moving backward." I suppose sitting still and idling is a third option, but that's not great, either. As author Marshall Goldsmith lays out in his fantastic book *What Got You Here, Won't Get You There*, every person, every leader, every company has a recipe for success that has helped them win and get ahead in life. Right up until the point it doesn't.

From the beginning, we acknowledged the need to get better continually and learn more both as individuals and as a team, and that desire has helped us succeed more than any of our other values. Unlike many leaders who define themselves by always being the smartest person in the room and "knowing everything," we try to take a learner mentality, to be challenged continually by the things we don't know. Our agency maintains an inquisitive spirit and takes pride in our relentless desire to learn, eat, see, hear, and experience new things. We recognize there is no finish line, and even when you're named Best in Show, Agency of the Year, or among the Best Places to Work, tomorrow morning the sun will come up and it will be time to start again.

UNITY—We Are Unified by Our Shared Commitments

Whether it's family, your alma mater, your favorite sports team, or the company you work for, we're all unified by the things we're committed to. Ever met a total stranger and found you have something in common? It completely changes your perspective and level of trust. We are all unified by the commitments we share.

In an agency setting, our unity comes from standing shoulder to shoulder fighting the brand wars on behalf of our clients. Their successes are our successes, and their disappointments strike us as hard as they do in the corporate office. We work long and hard every day, every month, every year. But it's not the work alone that unifies us. It's the work we achieve together. The collaboration and the camaraderie. The late nights and early mornings. The complicated campaigns and two-hour turnarounds. It's weddings and divorces. It's births and deaths. It's working together long enough to watch our children grow from baby showers to college graduation. We are unified by our shared commitments and for us, that starts with the extraordinary values we live into together.

DOES CULTURE REALLY MATTER THAT MUCH?

The answer to whether culture is really that important to success is like the answer to whether oxygen is key to survival. It's not. Unless you want to breathe.

As a leader, you have the power—and the responsibility—to author and oversee a culture that inspires, excites, empowers, and drives those who follow you to reach farther than their dreams allow. If you don't, who will?

Great culture has to come from the top down. It's the vision for how you want your team to treat your clients, your customers, your vendors and each other. Without a clearly defined culture and an unyielding accountability for buy-in, Zappos would be just another online retailer. Chick-fil-A would have good food with a fraction of the following. The Container Store, Pixar, Whole Foods, Southwest Airlines? They wouldn't be half the companies they are now.

There's a legendary story about the upscale retailer Nordstrom and a set of tires that frames the power of culture beautifully. As the story goes, in the 1970s, a man came into a Nordstrom store in Alaska to return a set of defective tires that he had purchased there. For those unfamiliar with Nordstrom, it's a department store. A really nice department store with men's and women's sections, a perfume and makeup counter, all kinds of accessories, home goods, and an unmatched shoe department. They've got everything, including a legendary culture for exemplary customer service. But they don't sell tires.

As the customer insisted that he had purchased the tires at that Nordstrom and now wanted to return them, there were a hundred things the sales associate could have said to explain how that was impossible. But he didn't. The Nordstrom associate took the tires and gave the man his money back. It was clear to the associate that Nordstrom didn't sell tires. But that didn't matter. The customer was sure he had purchased the tires there, and as far as the associate was concerned, the only right thing to do was take care of the customer. If the response had been, "I'm sorry sir, but Nordstrom doesn't sell tires," nobody ever would have heard the story. But because that associate lived into Nordstrom's ethos of taking care of their customers no matter what, we're still talking about it fifty years later.

That's the power of culture.

◇◇◇◇◇◇

FOOTNOTES

[1] Tony Hsieh, *Delivering Happiness: A Path To Profits, Passion and Purpose* (New York, NY: Grand Central Publishing, 2010), 157.

9

◇◇◇◇◇◇

READY FOR PRIMETIME

*Taking an Unflinching Look in the Mirror
and Making Difficult Adjustments*

In the last chapter, we talked about how building and curating your company's culture has to start with you. But before you can start building, you first need to take an unflinching look in the mirror and answer honestly whether you're up for the task. You may not be ready to lead your company. How's that for unflinching?

Don't misread that. It's not that you may be unfit to lead. You just may not be ready yet. Unfortunately, culture isn't the kind of thing that can materialize with the snap of your fingers, or a two-day planning meeting. It takes time. It takes thoughtful planning. And at its foundation, it takes a leader who's willing to look in the mirror honestly and identify the leadership strengths and weaknesses that will make your culture, your company, and your brand easier or harder to build.

Some people are just inherently good leaders. Born leaders as it's said. But for most of us—those without any formal leadership training, or lacking an honest, unflinching examination of what we do well and where we are falling short—leadership is a learning experience and one that can be a struggle because we don't recognize where our blind spots are. Think about your own leadership style. Would the team you're leading say you have a solid grasp on what you're doing well and where you're coming up short? Do *you* have a solid grasp on what you're doing well and where you're coming up short? And if so, how often do you think about those things? Once a quarter? Once a year during the company management retreat? Once or twice a year isn't enough.

Once a day probably isn't enough.

◇◇◇◇◇◇

LOOKING FOR YOUR BLIND SPOTS

Before any of us can be effective leaders, build cultures, or create brands, we first have to take an honest look at ourselves and acknowledge where we're effective and where we're lacking. For a lot of leaders, once they get to the CEO's chair, the president's chair, or the director's chair, there's a sense of arrival that comes with it. All the years of hard work, all the reading, all the ebbs and flows of ability have led you to this place and time where finally you are at the top and in charge of everything. For many, that arrival comes with a tendency to stop pushing yourself. To stop questioning what works and what doesn't. Your formula for success was good enough to get you to the top, so why change it?

You might be shocked at how many leaders we've met over the years in every possible category who were essentially tone deaf and oblivious to how ineffective their management style really was. Being the one in charge doesn't automatically make you the smartest person in the room. If you've hired well and created a great culture, that should almost never be the case. The best leaders understand that not every word that comes out of their mouths is gold, and not every idea is fantastic. That's not to say they don't take the mantle and lead the way. They do. But they're also not intimidated by other perspectives, even when they are contrary to their own. Leadership isn't ignoring or covering up the things you don't do well. It's understanding where your shortcomings lie and then filling those gaps with the talent around you.

You, as a leader, are not scalable.

That's why surrounding yourself with smart, energized, hard-working people is crucial to your growth. It's why building and maintaining a culture where those people can thrive is non-negotiable. And it's why taking an unflinching look at yourself and your company and making the tough decisions necessary to strengthen your weaknesses is the only chance you have to create and sustain excellence over time. If you're willing to do all of those things, you are lightyears ahead of most leaders and, better yet, you're primed to create something fantastic.

◇◇◇◇◇◇

DIFFERENT OPINIONS MAKE YOU STRONGER, NOT WEAKER

There's a funny story about Ron Polk, the legendary baseball coach at Mississippi State University, and a game he was coaching at the University of Arkansas. From the first pitch, Polk wasn't happy about the way the umpire was calling balls and strikes, and, after a few innings of frustration, he started tuning up and letting the ump know how he felt about his failing eyesight. At some point, the umpire had heard enough of Polk's chirping and threw him out of the game. Incensed, Polk stormed out of the dugout and started yelling at the ump, who quickly told him to get off the field. When Polk asked where the umpire expected him to go, he said, "I don't care. Just go someplace where I can't see you!" So, Polk went and stood on home plate.

Besides being hilarious, the story is a great reminder that smart, well-intentioned, educated people can look at the same exact situation and see two completely different things. As the leader of your company, or the director of your brand, it's logical to default to your own thoughts, views, ideas, and perspectives as the default course of action. But for the best leaders, that's not automatically the case.

The magic of creating a culture where everyone is invited into the process of curating that culture is that leadership can come from anywhere and everywhere. Great suggestions come from unexpected places. Innovation flourishes in unexpected places. Creativity abounds from unexpected places. When your people feel safe to voice their opinions and toss out their ideas without the fear of repercussion, when they can speak truth to power in the spirit of authenticity and making everyone better, when the ego of a knower mentality is replaced with the inquisitive wonder of a learner mentality throughout your team, there is literally no limit to what you can accomplish.

◇◇◇◇◇◇

WHAT TOYS, CARS, FISH AND
SUPERHEROES HAVE IN COMMON

Since the debut of the movie *Toy Story* in 1995, no studio in Hollywood has enjoyed a greater track record than Pixar. Twenty-one movies in, as of this writing, Pixar's comprehensive box office gross is north of $7 billion with a per-film average of more than $348 million when adjusted for inflation, according to Box Office Mojo. That's extraordinary in Hollywood. Even the films at the tail-end of Pixar's earnings like *Coco, Brave, Ratatouille,* and *WALL-E* were critical successes earning more than $200 million each. So what is it that's so special about Pixar?

While you can certainly make a case for a small cadre of visionaries led by directors, writers, and leaders like John Lasseter, Pete Docter, Andrew Stanton, and Pixar head Ed Catmull, they would be the first to tell you that the genius of Pixar is collective. Not among them, but the hundreds of people who work for the studio.

Wait, how does that work? We all know that "too many cooks spoil the broth." Clearly, movie-making is a collaborative effort. But giving hundreds of people an opinion with the expectation that they'll actually be listened to while the production team is on the clock and holding to a budget? That sounds like chaos.

For the record, it also sounds like $348 million in ticket sales per film.

From its founding, the leaders at Pixar understood that while they had fantastic ideas, there was no cornering the market on creativity, or objective observations about what was or wasn't working with a character, a script, or an edit. One of the legendary stories about Pixar (albeit true) is that in 1994, as Pixar was putting the finishing touches on *Toy Story*, Lasseter, Docter, Stanton, and writer Joe Ranf went out for lunch to discuss what their next project should be. Over the course of a few hours, the four outlined characters and plots on a stack of cocktail napkins for what would become *A Bug's Life, Monsters Inc., Finding Nemo,* and *WALL-E*. A $50 lunch. $1.5 billion in ticket sales.

Clearly these guys are gifted writers and directors who could easily hire any team in animation to work on their projects and simply execute their vision. But that's not what Pixar is all about.

As Pixar head Ed Catmull notes in Daniel Coyle's fantastic book *The Culture Code*, "Building creative purpose isn't really about creativity. It's about building ownership, providing support, and aligning group energy toward the arduous, error-filled, ultimately fulfilling journey of making something new."[1] For Catmull, that's not just a nice idea. It's the foundation of every system Pixar has, every decision they make, and every success they enjoy.

Pixar has created a culture of safety and purpose where everyone is empowered to speak up with suggestions about how to improve the movies they make. It's also a culture of vulnerability where even when millions of dollars are at stake, leaders and followers alike aren't afraid to raise their hands and say, "This isn't working," or, "I don't know the answer," or, "I need help." They call them "BrainTrust" meetings, and everyone is invited.

What would that kind of freedom look like in your organization?

And, as the leader of the pack, how would you react to that kind of authentic feedback? Honestly, could you accept that amount of truth? If the answer is no, that's both brave and understandable. It's counter-intuitive for the leader of a company to take feedback from those with less experience, limited perspectives, and fewer responsibilities. And yet, giving those people a legitimate voice is one of the foundational pillars to building a great culture. It's the difference between renting and buying. People do things in rental cars and apartments they would never do in their own cars, or their homes. Why? Because when you own something, you're invested in it in a way you can't possibly replicate on the periphery.

∞∞∞∞∞

EVERY LEADER WILLING TO BE COMPLETELY TRANSPARENT, TAKE ONE STEP FORWARD

At the beginning of the chapter, we talked about the need to look into the mirror and make an honest assessment of the leader looking back at you and how difficult that really is. Often times, the truth hurts, or disappoints. But without it, you can't build a solid foundation for anything, most especially your culture.

In *The Culture Code*, Daniel Coyle lists building safety, sharing vulnerability, and establishing purpose as the three imperative skills every leader has to have to build an extraordinary culture. For most of us, safety and purpose make complete sense. But vulnerability? It's not much of a stretch to say, culturally, that vulnerability has long been associated with weakness. But nothing could be further from the truth.

At LOOMIS, we are huge fans of Brené Brown, the country's leading researcher in the area of vulnerability and the author of great reads like *Daring Greatly* and *Braving the Wilderness*. In her first TED Talk called "The Power Of Vulnerability" (one of the top five TED Talks of all time with more than 42 million views), Dr. Brown echoed why it's imperative for leaders to lean into their vulnerability. In describing the revelations that came from her research, she said, "I know that vulnerability is the core of shame and fear and our struggle for worthiness. But, it appears, it's also the birthplace of joy, of creativity, of belonging, of love."

When leaders allow themselves to be vulnerable with the people they lead—not to have every answer, to ask for help, to make mistakes and own up to them—they are not exposing weakness. They are exuding authenticity and *that* is what people are drawn to. Vulnerability sparks cooperation and trust. Think about your most intimate relationships. Without vulnerability, those relationships wouldn't be a fraction of what they are, nor would they be as meaningful. In a similar way, the relationships you foster with your team and your ability to move them forward is in large part predicated on your ability to be genuine with them without the fear of being taken advantage of. Admittedly, a tall order for most of us.

When we think about vulnerability and leaping into the unknown, we normally think of first building trust, then leaping. But it turns out, we need to do the opposite. As Coyle points out, "Science shows that when it comes to creating cooperation, vulnerability is not a risk, but a psychological requirement."[2] Letting your guard down and allowing for "exchanges of vulnerability" creates connection. And that's the foundation for everything.

FOOTNOTES

[1] Daniel Coyle, *The Culture Code* (New York, NY: Bantam Books, 2018), 226.

[2] Ibid, 111.

10

◇◇◇◇◇◇

IT'S NOT ABOUT FOOSBALL—THE REAL ELEMENTS OF GREAT CULTURE

What makes a company a great place to work?

Like most questions, the answer largely depends on who you ask. Ping pong tables and foosball are fun. Open concept floor plans with hanging chairs, endless bowls of chocolate, and white board walls you can write on? Trendy and cool. How about a round bamboo Zen room with low lighting, trickling water, and a quiet sitar soundtrack where you can go to decompress when the stress gets to be too much? Not lying, that one sounds awesome.

There are health-conscious companies that order in gourmet lunches and dinners every day, companies with built-in gyms and sleeping areas so you never actually have to go home, and more places than you'd think where people ride bicycles and Segways around the halls. There are companies with snack closets so robust you wouldn't be shocked to see a Costco employee there handing out samples. And more than a few with Kegerators on tap 24/7. All in the spirit of improving morale, driving productivity, and attracting top-notch talent.

No doubt, these things are fun and cool. But they're also just distractions. Depending on the employee, they may get someone in the door, but alone, they're not going to keep them. Great culture runs deeper than that and, not surprisingly, so does great talent.

⬦⬦⬦⬦⬦⬦

MOVING BEYOND COOL

The introductory premise of Daniel Coyle's landmark book *The Culture Code* is that "culture is not something you are. It's something you do."[1] In other words, culture is active. And when it comes to great company cultures, it's not the superficial we respond to, but something far more primal. That explains why shiny objects like Margarita Mondays, freshly baked cookies every afternoon, and Friday afternoon chair massages aren't the building blocks of lasting company cultures, as enjoyable as they are. Great companies are built on elements that speak to us on a far deeper, more meaningful level than momentary gratification ever could.

In *The Culture Code*, Coyle lists safety, vulnerability, and purpose as the three essential skills every leader must master to build a great culture. And while it's certainly true that extraordinary cultures can be built on those three elements alone, in the case of challenger brands, we believe there are four additional elements that are essential to building a transcendent culture. To safety, vulnerability, and purpose, we add belonging, creativity, connection, and North Star leadership.

⬦⬦⬦⬦⬦⬦

THE (CULTURAL) MAGNIFICENT SEVEN

1. SAFETY

We've all heard that "blood is thicker than water." And when you talk to people who work in strong cultures, that's how they feel about the team they work with. Ask about their office relationships and you're just as likely to hear words like *friends* and *family* as you are *co-workers* or *fellow employees*. There's an implied emotional distance with those last two. But when people work side by side with those they consider "family," you can bet it's a place they feel safe both physically and psychologically. They can be vulnerable because they know people genuinely care about them. For those groups, cultivating the feeling of safety is no accident.

Strong company cultures regularly give off cues that tell people they are in a safe environment. And they have to. Just as it was when we were children, or later when we started developing more meaningful relationships, building up a sense of psychological safety and trust takes time, while destroying it can happen in an instant.

So how do you build a sense of safety? In a series of studies conducted by the MIT Human Dynamics Lab, they found that team performance is driven by five measurable factors:

1. Everyone in the group talks and listens in roughly equal measure, keeping contributions short.
2. Members maintain high levels of eye contact, and their conversations and gestures are energetic.
3. Members communicate directly with one another, not just with the team leader.

4. Members carry on back-channel or side conversations within the team.

5. Members periodically break, go exploring outside the team, and bring information back to share with the others.[2]

Think for a second how different that may be from the interactions you have with the people in your company. How much breathing room are you really giving them? Even as the leader, do you approach every meeting or conversation with the preconception that you have to be the smartest person in the room? Are you giving off belonging cues that say, "I trust what you're doing," "I value your opinion," and, "You are safe." Think about how distressing it must feel to work in an environment where the answer to those three questions is no.

If you're not reflecting safety cues in your own behavior, there's no way it's being reflected in your overall culture. It reminds me of one of my favorite quotes from Ralph Waldo Emerson: "Your actions speak so loudly, I cannot hear what you are saying."

So why is safety so important? Because it is. Whether conscious or unconscious, our preoccupation with feeling safe goes back to the very beginning. Our cave-dwelling ancestors fought the same anxieties we do—how to be productive, how to figure out what and who to trust, how to survive—and they were just as fixated as we are. As Robert Cialdini discusses in his book *Pre-Suasion: A Revolutionary Way to Influence and Persuade*, we give greater importance to the things we focus on to the point that we assign causality to them.[3] Is it any wonder that when we feel unsafe, it's the only thing we can think about?

In a work culture, feeling safe—or unsafe—colors how we feel about everything. If we want to build a strong, productive culture, our job as leaders is to create a place where our people feel safe to contribute openly. That doesn't mean building safe rooms for employees who can't handle tough feedback. On the contrary, it often means delivering brutal honesty and uncomfortable truths, but done in a way that leads with love and a signal that we're in this together and more importantly, that we share a future together.

2. VULNERABILITY

It's not a huge stretch to say that culturally, vulnerability has long been associated with weakness. But it shouldn't be. As we mentioned, we're big fans of Brené Brown, the country's leading researcher in the area of vulnerability and as we noted in the last chapter, in Dr. Brown's first TED Talk called "The Power of Vulnerability," she echoed why it's imperative for leaders to lean into their vulnerability. Again, in describing the revelations that came from her research, she said, "I know that vulnerability is the core of shame and fear and our struggle for worthiness. But, it appears, it's also the birthplace of joy, of creativity, of belonging, of love."[4]

In leadership, you can focus on yourself, or you can focus on your team and the task at hand. The question becomes how important are connectedness, cooperation, and opening yourself up? Surely with talented people, efficient systems, clear direction, and financial support, companies should have enough to succeed. And they do, assuming they're a company of one.

For teams of two or more, unparalleled excellence and

transcendent performance requires a closeness that comes from fearless vulnerability. Think about groups, teams, and ensembles that have exuded excellence for generations. Cirque du Soleil. The Yankees and Patriots. The New York Philharmonic. Army Rangers and Navy SEALs. That kind of elite, enduring performance could never be sustained with superficial connection and an absence of trust.

Think of your company and the people you lead. Do you share genuine connection, unbridled vulnerability, and complete trust, or are those completely foreign concepts? What about your team? Do they practice openness, honesty, and connection with you and with each other? If not, that is most certainly standing in the way of you and your team reaching your full promise. The good news? Lack of group vulnerability is fixable. All it takes is time, repetition, and the willingness to feel a little pain in order to move forward.

3. PURPOSE

In any organization, purpose isn't a *me* orientation. It's a *we* orientation. According to Coyle, "Purpose isn't about tapping into some mystical internal drive, but rather about creating simple beacons that focus attention and engagement on the shared goal."[5]

Purpose is the thing that gets us from where we are to where we want to go. It seems easy enough. But too often, purpose comes in the form of some top-down edict announcing grand intentions without the actions to back it up. Day in and day out, purpose isn't delivered with big, demonstrative actions, but rather with a countless number of small, vivid signals that say, "This is our vision," "We're in this together," and, "You are an important part of our future and our success." Is that what your leadership is saying to the people who work for you? I had the great fortune of working for a legendary CEO here in Dallas who was very intentional about making his employees feel valued.

When I was a young copywriter, my third job out of school was at a big agency in Dallas called Temerlin McClain. The agency was a conservative stalwart that employed more than seven hundred people working on blue chip accounts like American Airlines, JCPenney, Exxon Mobil, and Subaru. It was the biggest agency I've ever worked for.

At some point during my first few years at the agency, I learned that agency chairman and namesake Liener Temerlin was also heavily involved with the American Film Institute (AFI) in Los Angeles and was the creative force behind the initial AFI Top 100 movies list. As a huge movie fan, I would have loved nothing more than to spend hours talking movies with Liener. But as a young writer, unless I bumped into him somewhere in the agency, there was very little reason for us to interact. Fortunately for me, that did happen on occasion.

On one such morning, I found myself on the elevator with Liener and our conversation found its way to *Pulp Fiction* which had just been released. He thought it was "brilliant" and wondered if I had seen it yet. Liener loved all movies, but after discussing what was new, he always loved educating me about the "old" movies I needed to see. "Have you seen *The Swimmer* with Burt Lancaster?" he'd ask. "It's fantastic! Gotta see that. What about *Mr. Skeffington* with Bette Davis and Claude Rains? No? You've got to see that."

With every conversation, I would take copious mental notes

about all the movies I needed to watch, but unfortunately, even in the heyday of Blockbuster, black and white, non-Oscar winners from 1944 weren't always available for rental.

About a week later, my phone rang. It was Liener's assistant. "Mr. Temerlin would like to see you in his office," she said. I can still hear her voice and remember wondering what in the world I'd done wrong to warrant a trip to the chairman's office. When I got up to the ninth floor where all the executives sat, Liener's assistant told me he was expecting me and to go on in. I knocked on his door, and Liener told me to have a seat.

Smiling, he reached around behind his desk and grabbed a black plastic bag. He stuck his hand inside and tossed me a VHS tape wrapped in cellophane. I turned it over and there was a picture of Bette Davis smiling up at me. It was *Mr. Skeffington*. "I was at the mall yesterday," he said, "I saw that and thought of you." I literally had no words.

In that moment, I knew just about everything I needed to know about Liener Temerlin's character and that of the agency he built. At that point, I had spoken to the man half a dozen times in my life. I was a small fish in a very big pond and yet he was thoughtful enough to do something special—for me. In that moment, and every day of his career, Liener Temerlin embodied the purpose of his agency. To take extraordinary care of his clients and the people who worked for him. Purpose isn't about grand gestures and big promises. It's about living into what you say is most important to you every day. It's about how you treat the people you choose to go to battle with. I no longer own a VCR. But I'll have that copy of *Mr. Skeffington* for the rest of my life.

What stories are you telling yourself about the people you work with? What assumptions are you making that consciously and unconsciously affect the way you interact with those you lead? How you encourage them, isolate them, push them, hold them back? When you rally people around purpose—when you live into purpose—it requires complete buy in. Not just from them, but from you. If building extraordinary culture takes things like safety, vulnerability, purpose, belonging, creativity, and collaboration, those things have to flow both ways and they must be reflected in everything you do. Anything less is just pretending.

4. BELONGING

How important is a sense of belonging to building a fantastic culture? When was the last time you chose to stay in a place where you didn't feel accepted, connected, loved, or valued? Those feelings are bellwethers for isolation and divorce, not belonging and relationship. At our core, we all want to belong and to be appreciated and included. In Maslow's Hierarchy of Needs, love and belonging lie just below the pinnacle of esteem and self-actualization and, yet, we can't reach the last two without first feeling loved and accepted.

Belonging is primal. And no matter how introverted any of us may be, belonging isn't optional. It's required for life and everything that goes with it. In 2017, *Business Insider* posted a story from *Inc.* that quoted a clinical review of nearly 150 studies covering more than 300,000 people that concluded that people with strong social ties—that is, close friendships—"had a fifty percent better chance of survival, regardless of age, sex, health status, and cause of death than those with weaker ties."[6]

It goes without saying that belonging and the need for intimacy, love, and connection are crucial to our private lives, but it goes much further than that. Statistically, we spend half of our waking hours at work, and our need to belong isn't something we can just cut off when we leave home and head to the office. Part of building a meaningful, productive culture means creating an environment where people feel welcome and accepted and part of a tribe that appreciates them and has their back.

Belonging isn't about fitting in, or acclimating. It's about genuine connection. When people feel a bond and a friendship with their co-workers, they stay. They work harder. They contribute more. When they don't, they either leave (bad), or they stay and fester; unhappy, unconnected, and unfulfilled (worse).

In 2017, LinkedIn posted a piece on their TalentBlog that listed what more than fourteen thousand global professionals said gave them a sense of belonging at work. The top 10 included:

1. Being recognized for my accomplishments (59%)
2. Having opportunities to express my opinions freely (51%)
3. Feeling that my contributions in team meetings are valued (50%)
4. Feeling comfortable with being myself at work (50%)
5. Transparent communication about important company developments (48%)
6. Feeling like my team/company cares about me as a person (46%)
7. Feedback on my personal growth (39%)
8. Being assigned work deemed important for the team/ company (39%)

9. Having the company values align with my own personal values (37%)

10. Being a part of important company meetings (24%)[7]

Look beneath the surface of these responses, and belonging looks a lot like a want for acceptance and inclusion in an environment that's free of fear and open to diversity. Is that what your company looks like? How many of these things would your employees say are true about the culture you've built? What signals of belonging (or not belonging) are you sending to the people who work for you? The number one reason people stay, or leave a company is their relationship with the person directly above them. If they feel like they belong, they'll line up and follow you anywhere. If not, they're as good as gone.

5. CREATIVITY

Thinking something into existence where once there was nothing. That's the essence of creativity. Einstein called it "intelligence having fun." Unless you're running an accounting firm, creativity is essential for growing your company and, even in the case of accountants, it's foundational to building and maintaining a lasting culture. Just picture what a company would look like, feel like, and act like if it was completely devoid of creativity.

Imagine you're in the market to buy a restaurant, or to eat at a restaurant, or to get a job working for a restaurant. You narrow it down to two. The first is solid. Good food, good service, never had a bad meal, but the menu never changes. The second is equally good, but there's always something new going on. Interesting dinner specials. New cocktails. Specially themed, invitation-only sampling parties for loyal customers. There's always something that's just... fresh. Which restaurant are you drawn to?

In 2007, the market research firm Yankelovich estimated the average person living in a city was exposed to five thousand ad messages a day.[8] With the explosion of digital media, it's safe to say that number has increased, but whether it's by one thousand, five thousand, or ten thousand, it still begs the same questions—Which messages do you notice? Which ads are you drawn to? Which commercials do you actually like and tell your friends about? It's not the spots for personal injury attorneys, pharmaceuticals, or car dealerships.

There's a reason we like the GEICO gecko and the Chick-fil-A cows and the little boy in the Darth Vader costume trying to start his father's Volkswagen with his special powers. It's the same reason Pixar averages $348 million per film when other animated movies come and go in a matter of days. As thinking, feeling beings we are drawn to what's smart, what's emotional, and what's creative. Your company culture is no different.

Why do people hang out at Starbucks rather than a hospital waiting room? They both have chairs and coffee. Your team spends eight to twelve hours a day working on your company's behalf. They need a place where they can create. Try something new. Head in new directions with the freedom to fail and try again.

Every great culture embraces creativity. Talented people need an open-minded commitment to push for something smarter, cooler and newer. They want a culture that's fresh and exciting and something they can be an intricate part of. To compete and thrive, challenger brands especially have to do things differently. Where glacial brands can chug along with the status quo, challengers need to be creative in everything they do. And they have to make "What if?" and "Why not?" an intrinsic part of their dialogue and their culture. Creativity can be a game changer. The question is, are you willing to open the box?

6. CONNECTION

The sixth essential element to building a transcendent culture is connection. It's a close cousin to belonging but where a sense of belonging is more emotional, or spiritual, connection is more physical. It's measured in friendships, mentors, relationships, and second families. Connection happens when people are included, when they're trusted, when they are invited to be part of something bigger than themselves. It happens when people buy into leadership, into the company ethos, and into what makes your brand special and unlike any other.

Kip Tindell says "communication is leadership." Communication builds connection. When your employees feel connected and believe in both you and each other, jobs become careers and careers become callings. If you're a challenger brand, connection is something you should foster every day while size works to your advantage. With the right people in place, the tighter your bond, the faster you can grow. Albeit, with one caveat—the connection has to be real.

We live in an era when too many people measure their level of connection in likes and retweets and shared posts and Facebook friends. Genuine connection is about physically doing life—and business—with people you love and trust. In many companies, that's easier said than done. But when you get it right, people stick. At LOOMIS, we've gotten plenty wrong over the years but when it comes to connection, we seem to have done a pretty good job. Since 1999, our average tenure of employment is 7.6 years—more than twice the ad industry average. But we also recognize that if our culture was left untended, people wouldn't want to stay. And with more and more Millennials and Gen Z entering the workforce every day, workplace culture and fostering real connection is more important than ever. Here's why.

For both millennials (aka Gen Y) and Gen Z (those born after 1995), loneliness is epidemic, and not for many of the reasons you might think like cell phones and social media. According to the 2018 Cigna U.S. Loneliness Index, eighteen- to twenty-two-year-olds are the loneliest generation in America, even more than our nation's elderly.[9] That backs up what a landmark UCLA study uncovered in 2015:

- According to UCLA's 2015 Freshman Survey that included responses from 150,000 full-time students at more than 200 colleges and universities, over the past ten years, the number of first-year students who spent sixteen or more hours a week hanging out with friends fell by nearly half to eighteen percent.
- The same survey showed that forty-one percent of students said they felt "overwhelmed by all I had to do" and logged the highest levels of unhappiness ever recorded among women.
- The study found that sixty-nine percent of the age group felt

the people around them were "not really with them" and sixty-eight percent felt as if no one knew them well. [10]

Digging a little deeper into the Cigna study:

- Approximately one in six adults in the U.S. suffer from a mental health condition, and research has noted that mental health issues are one of the most rapidly increasing causes of long-term sick leave. When examining the different issues affecting people with mental health conditions, there is a consistent part of the pathology: they also suffer from loneliness.
- Loneliness has the same impact on mortality as smoking fifteen cigarettes a day, making it even more dangerous than obesity.
- Generation Z (ages 18-22) and millennials (ages 23-37) are lonelier and claim to be in worse health than older generations. [11]

Consider for a second, the first six essentials for building a meaningful culture: safety, vulnerability, purpose, belonging, creativity, and connection. Can you think of any six things that a generation suffering from loneliness and overwhelm need more than that? Can you think of any six things that *you* need more than that?

We have the ability to create that kind of culture in our own companies. Imagine for a second a place where we foster inclusion and diversity and where we show empathy and genuine concern for the people we work with. A place where we're transparent, open, and, when necessary, apologetic. A place where we manage with purpose, live our values, lead by example and place ethics above all else. We have it in our power to create that kind of environment. And when we do, we won't just attract these super talented young people who are determined to make us better. We'll connect with them. We'll thrive with them in a loving, supportive, collaborative environment. And we'll actually hang on to them.

7. NORTH STAR LEADERSHIP

The seventh essential element for building a transcendent culture is North Star Leadership. Admittedly, there's not a more hackneyed, amorphous word in all of business than leadership. And yet, it's something we desperately need more of. For some people, natural, effective leadership seems to be something they're born with while, for most of us, it takes a lifetime of learning, soul-searching, and mistakes. In the end, our ability to lead our companies is what we will all be measured by. All the more reason to learn as much as we can from those who are routinely recognized as extraordinary leaders.

Every year in April, *TIME Magazine* puts out their "100 Most Influential People" issue and every year, we're fascinated. About who made the list, why they were chosen, and how, from the 7.53 billion people on the planet, these one hundred people became the leaders we look to for influence. Each year, *TIME* includes world leaders, scientists, activists, entertainers, conservationists, and disruptors. Or, as *TIME* classifies them, Pioneers, Artists, Leaders, Titans, and Icons.

Each leader in the issue gets one hundred to two hundred words written about them by someone who knows them. And while there are only a handful of mentions about the direct influence these leaders had on their organization's culture, put in the context of our essential building blocks, every description highlights a consistent set of leadership traits congruent with extraordinary cultures. What's fascinating is that none of the traits are superhuman. They're traits you and I have complete access to every day. Is it possible that exceptional leadership hinges as much on how we are, as who we are? The 2019 *TIME* 100 would certainly suggest the answer is yes.

◇◇◇◇◇◇

THE PIONEERS[12]

Included among the 2019 Pioneers: Sandra Oh, Fred Swaniker, Chrissy Teigen, Lynn Nottage, Naomi Osaka, Aileen Lee, Marlon James, and Indya Moore.

These are the groundbreakers. The disruptors. The people who are about anything but the status quo. This is the group who saw the way the world worked and said, "You know what? I don't think so." And while you may expect the descriptions of their leadership styles to be equally edgy and uncompromising, they're not. They're hopeful, inspiring, and creative. Words like *virtuoso, undeniable, nuanced, fearless, approachable, compassion, empathy, honest, polite, self-deprecating*, and *brilliant* are used time and time again. It turns out this group is less about destroying the world that was and more focused on creating a new one that's better.

THE ARTISTS[13]

Included among the 2019 Artists: Dwayne Johnson, Ariana Grande, Regina King, Emilia Clarke, Mahershala Ali, and Chip and Joanna Gaines.

The lonely, isolated, tortured artist is a long-standing trope that would have you believe beauty can only come from introverted talent mired in pain. And while that may be true for some artists, the ones we hold up as leaders seem to be the exact opposite. Each is described as giving, loving, and more concerned with others than themselves. Those who know them best describe them with words like *warmth, positivity, genuine, resilient, changing the game, courage, stamina, captivating, soulful, vulnerable, generous*, and *unassuming*. The lesson these artists teach? Creating something beautiful and lasting starts with thinking of others first.

THE LEADERS[14]

Included among the 2019 Leaders: Nancy Pelosi, Donald Trump, Jane Goodall, Xi Jinping, Robert Mueller, Benjamin Netanyahu, and Pope Francis.

Think back on your career and the worst leaders you've ever worked for. What descriptors come to mind? *Arrogant. Inflexible. Unfair. Tone-deaf.* Now think about the best leaders you've

IT'S NOT ABOUT FOOSBALL | 137

worked for and what words describe them. *Visionary. Supportive. Empathetic. Inspiring.* Too often, when people find themselves in charge—especially for the first time—they lean into how they think a person in charge is supposed to act rather than what's actually effective. And yet consider that the tribute writers for *TIME* described the most influential leaders in the world with words like *driving force, confidence, presence, optimism, unwavering commitment, legacy, benevolence, virtue, duty, integrity, humility, courage,* and *wisdom*. Perhaps it's true what they say. If you want to be the best, learn from the best.

◇◇◇◇◇◇

THE TITANS[15]

Included among the 2019 Titans: Mohammed Salah, Jeanne Gang, Ryan Murphy, Jerome Powell, LeBron James, Alex Morgan, Tiger Woods, and Bob Iger.

It would be understandable to believe the further up the food chain a leader goes, the more controlling and dictatorial they will become. After all, they are most likely the ones with the vision, and quite certainly the ones responsible for making sure the vision—for the company, for the film, for the conglomerate, for the career—becomes reality. That kind of responsibility and pressure often brings out the darker palette of leadership traits. And yet, again, when you look at the titans at the top of their form, they're not remembered as, or described by adjectives that are, the least bit negative, critical, or self-centered. Rather, those who know these titans best describe them as *iconic, humble, thoughtful, a catalyst for change, childlike enthusiasm, boundless imagination, born storyteller, accountable, grounded, fearless, patient,* and *curious.* Not sure the correlation between positive, affirming, supportive leadership and a greater rate of success can be much clearer.

∞∞∞∞

THE ICONS[16]

Included among the 2019 Icons: Taylor Swift, Spike Lee, Desmond Meade, Christine Blasey Ford, Lady Gaga, and Michelle Obama.

Of the millions of leaders who have ever left their mark in the arena of competition, very few ever reach the rarefied air of being called an icon. To be included in that group requires vision and leadership that transcends the good, the great, or even the exceptional. And while you may think that level of leadership looks extraordinarily different, it doesn't really. The same adjectives used to describe the other pioneers, artists, leaders, and titans on *TIME*'s Top 100 Influencers list also describe those "once in a generation" leaders we call icons. Words like *honest, raw, electrifying, a model, visionary, original, courage, undaunted, committed, inventive, outrageous, inner strength, regal, reassuring,* and *calm.*

∞∞∞∞

SO, HOW ARE YOU?

Is it possible that exceptional leadership hinges as much on *how* we are, as *who* we are? As much? No. Exceptional leadership has *everything* to do with how we are. And so does building a culture that will not only attract the best talent, but keep them for years to come. It's not easy and it takes an extraordinary, sustained amount of attention, focus, and effort. But when you can build a company with safety, vulnerability, purpose, belonging, creativity, connection, and leadership at its core, there are few who will ever be able to challenge you.

○○○○○○

FOOTNOTES

[1] Daniel Coyle, *The Culture Code* (New York, NY: Bantam Books, 2018), xx.

[2] Ibid, 14-15.

[3] Robert Cialdini, *Pre-Suasion: A Revolutionary Way to Influence and Persuade* (New York, NY: Simon & Schuster, 2016), 51.

[4] Brené Brown, "The Power of Vulnerability," Jan. 3, 2011. YouTube.

[5] Coyle, *The Culture Code*, 180.

[6] Jeff Haden, "A Study of 300,000 People Found Living a Longer, Happier Life Isn't Just about Diet, Exercise, or Genetics," *Inc.*, Oct. 21, 2017.

[7] Maxwell Huppert, "Employees Share What Gives Them A Sense of Belonging At Work," LinkedIn Business Solutions, Oct. 25, 2017.

[8] Louise Story, "Anywhere the Eye Can See, It's Likely to See an Ad," *New York Times*, Jan. 15, 2007.

[9] 2018 Cigna U.S. Loneliness Index, Sept. 10, 2019.

[10] The American Freshman: National Norms Fall 2015, Sept. 10, 2019.

[11] 2018 Cigna U.S. Loneliness Index, Sept. 10, 2019.

[12] "The 100 Most Influential People," *TIME*, April 29/May 6, 2019, 25-52.

[13] Ibid, 53-74.

[14] Ibid, 75-104.

[15] Ibid, 105-120.

[16] Ibid, 121-134.

THE CUSTOMER RESPONSE

Starting With the End in Mind

Thus far, we've talked a lot about the importance of building a meaningful culture, the environment and the feelings culture creates, as well as how culture can both positively and negatively affect the people who work in your company. But that's all inward facing. What happens when that culture reaches your company's front door, or the company homepage, or your brand's product facing in the grocery store? What happens when internal culture meets external customer?

Building a transcendent culture is imperative to building a lasting brand. But that effort is never one of sheer benevolence, ego, or vanity. Building a great company or a great brand is always in service to a customer transaction in the outside world whether it's selling products, serving customers, or aiding humanity. And as much as some companies might want a mutually exclusive relationship between their internal culture and external brand, there is an inherently osmotic effect that precludes that from being possible.

Think about your office. No matter what role your people play in building your brand, every day, every week, 2,500-3,000 hours a year, your team consciously (and subconsciously) soaks in every aspect of their environment. And, as a result, how your team feels about your company and your leadership bleeds into everything they do. Everything. How products are designed, how they're manufactured, how they're shipped, and how they're marketed and sold. How food is prepared in a restaurant, how closely recipes are followed, what kind of service is provided, and in what kind of environment. Even in a cause-based non-profit with real life and death consequences, how the team is conditioned has everything to do with the effectiveness of their effort.

The brand and the culture you build are inextricably linked to the experience you deliver to your end consumer. That experience can be unbelievably positive. But it can also be catastrophically negative. The good news is that you have control over how that narrative unfolds. All you have to do is start with the end of the story in mind and build the brand and culture that will bring about the result you want.

To see what that looks like, consider three extraordinary examples of global brands that were meticulously built over the last ten, twenty, and forty years. They all live in the same general space, they all transcended their category, and they all exponentially exceeded expectations that were already through the roof. You might recognize them if you've ever spent any time in space, a galaxy far, far away, or a little place called Westeros.

◇◇◇◇◇◇

CREATING A SUPERHUMAN BRAND EXPERIENCE

When *Avengers: End Game* hit theaters in April 2019, it brought an end to Phase Three of the Marvel Cinematic Universe (MCU) and concluded the most extraordinary, interconnected run in the history of the movies. Think of any cinematic touchstone in your lifetime. From a financial standpoint, from a technological standpoint, or from a branding standpoint, there's never been anything quite like the twenty-two-film tapestry that comprised the MCU. Ironically, the only things that even come close in their breadth, quality of production, and number of rabid fans are *Game of Thrones* and *Star Wars*, which also concluded their runs in the same year. 2019 was a tough year to be a nerd.

Joking aside, there's no better way to describe the MCU, *Game of Thrones*, and *Star Wars* than by calling them phenomena. And while it would be easy to characterize all three series as geeky, fantasy fare, the truth is, they didn't get where they are just because of the Comic-Con crowd. They flourished because they captured the rest of us, making those who wouldn't ordinarily pay attention sit up and take notice. How? By picturing their ultimate end game experience and then building the brands that could deliver it. Consider these numbers:

The Marvel Cinematic Universe:
- Twenty-two films
- $3.91 billion spent on production[1]
- $8.56 billion in domestic box office[1]
- $21.45 billion in worldwide box office[1]

HBO's Game of Thrones:

- Seventy-three episodes
- Broadcast in 207 countries and territories
- Season One average viewers – 9.3 million[2]
- Season Eight average viewers – 44 million[2]
- 161 Primetime Emmy nominations with 59 wins[3]

Star Wars:

- Twelve films
- $1.58 billion spent on production[4]
- $4.56 billion in domestic box office[5]
- $9.49 billion in worldwide box office[5]

The numbers are astounding and there's not a brand on the planet that wouldn't love to have the success and fan loyalty these franchises command. That may seem like an impossible task, but consider this: in 1975, George Lucas's claim to fame was a love letter to the '50s called *American Graffiti*. In 2007, the MCU only existed in comic books. In 2010, *A Game of Thrones* was a single book in the fantasy section of the bookstore.

Once upon a time, these behemoths were all challenger brands. But they started with the end in mind and a vision for what they wanted to be and what they wanted to deliver to the consumer.

That's not to say all the details were planned out because, clearly, they weren't. But each of these franchises knew the customer experience they wanted to deliver and then built their brands accordingly. All three took different and circuitous routes to success. But if you look closely, you can see they all leaned hard into five tenets of challenger branding that ultimately set them apart from everything else that looked or felt remotely like them. These tenets aren't tied to fantasy or science fiction or even filmmaking. They're five challenger brand pillars that can serve any brand well. All it takes is having the forethought, courage, and discipline to see them through.

5 FOUNDATIONAL TENETS FOR BUILDING YOUR CHALLENGER BRAND

1. START WITH GREAT STORYTELLING

Over a century of filmmaking, there have been thousands of movies and television shows in the fantasy/sci-fi genre, but none connected like Marvel, *Game of Thrones*, and *Star Wars*, and that begins and ends with their extraordinary storytelling, not their production value.

With the media you have at your fingertips (both old and new) there has never been a better time to tell broad, fantastic, integrated stories. And yet, for most brands, story is an afterthought. Or worse, a never thought. If you truly want to connect with your customers, tell great stories in smart, touching, funny, dramatic, engaging ways. That goes for the brand itself and, if you're a marketer, for the advertising you create. Engaging storytelling is the most ancient and effective method we have to connect people. Tell your story well and people will notice.

2. THINK AHEAD AND PLAN ACCORDINGLY

A twenty-two-film story arc doesn't happen by accident. The MCU is an inspired, perfectly-planned universe of character and crossover that becomes even more brilliant when you go back and watch it from the beginning. The same can be said for the *Game of Thrones* and *Star Wars* sagas.

Whether it's due to timing, budget, or lack of imagination, most brands shy away from this kind of broad production, opting instead to produce single spots or, at best, limited campaigns that rarely build on each other. Like compound interest in financing, great ideas that advance an intriguing narrative are far more lucrative than ones that are simply one and done. Think in interactive campaigns rather than spots and your impact could be exponential.

3. REMEMBER, LOVE MAKES THE BRAND GO AROUND

There are literally millions of people who know about Marvel, *Game of Thrones*, and *Star Wars* who have never seen a single episode or film. Why? Because those brands have intersected all of our lives in numerous and unexpected places. In part, that's due to smart licensing and brand crossover (have you had the *Game of Thrones* Oreos?) But the bigger reason is that, early on, fans connected with these franchises because of story and character and production and humor. Lovers of these brands felt a sense of community, took ownership, and became a PR machine one hundred million strong.

Theirs was not a passive affection. It was the kind of rabid, all-consuming love that drove millions of people to buy tickets for the opening night of *Infinity War, End Game*, and *The Last Jedi* months in advance. It's a love that drove millions of people to rewatch the entire *Game of Thrones* series for the seventh time, just to prepare for Season Eight. Brand lovers become loyalists, and loyalists become evangelists. Give your customers authentic reasons to love you and they will. Then they'll tell everybody they know how much.

4. MAKE AN EMOTIONAL CONNECTION

Is it harder to evoke emotion in a thirty-second TV commercial, a magazine print ad, or a brand website than a two-hour movie? Sure. But for too many brands, that's become an excuse to stop trying. Tapping into genuine emotion is what binds us together as human beings. In truth, it might be the only thing. When we experience the world in a way that makes us feel—happy, sad, amused, or heartbroken—that experience chemically implants the experience in our brain. That's why we can all remember exactly where we were the morning of 9/11 or how we felt the moment our children were born.

Brands that evoke emotion have the same power. If you're an avid fantasy fan, think how you felt when Thanos snapped his fingers at the end of *Avengers: Infinity War*; in the final moments of the Red Wedding in season three of *Game of Thrones*; or when Darth Vader looked at Luke in *The Empire Strikes Back* and said, "No, I am your father." Find genuine emotional touchpoints for your brand and use them. Their impact echoes.

5. ANCHOR THE BRAND IN REAL LIFE EXPERIENCES

By definition, fantasy is anything but real. As much as we might want, none of us can fly or ride a dragon or wield a light saber apart from our own imaginations. But that's why we watch. We love seeing those things on screen. They're fun and amazing and all part of our temporary departure from the real world. But they're also only half of the equation. The reason Marvel, *Game of Thrones*, and *Star Wars* are what they are is because at their core, they are grounded in humanity. They're steeped in real life experience, and, because of that, we see ourselves in them.

Smart branding works the same way. Great creativity grounded in real life experience—love, hate, life, death, argument, resolution, thoughtfulness, care, loneliness, redemption—helps people connect the dots. It grounds your brand in something familiar, and it holds up a mirror that allows people to see themselves. Like running into a good friend, people pay attention to what they recognize. They stop, focus, and trade their most precious commodity, time, for a moment of connection. That's where genuine brand loyalty starts. And, as we all know, that's the first step toward ruling the universe.

◇◇◇◇◇◇

SO HOW DO I KNOW WHAT THE END LOOKS LIKE?

Understanding what you really want your brand to be about begins and ends with the story you want to tell. Think about your brand as if it's a movie genre. Is it a drama? A comedy? A love story? A historical documentary? Let's hope it's not a tragedy. For a lot of companies, you can see the brand narrative reflected in their taglines.

Nike: "Just Do It" (Stop talking, stop making excuses, get up and move.)

Apple: "Think Different" (Products for people who are anything but status quo.)

FedEx: "Relax, it's FedEx" (Worry-free shipping.)

Hallmark: "When You Care Enough To Send The Very Best" (All other greeting cards are inferior.)

Allstate: "You're In Good Hands" (We've got you covered.)

The truth is, you may or may not have a good handle on what your brand story is. Either way, you're not alone. If you understand your story, good for you. Dig deep. Find ways to expand it and to bring it to life. If, on the other hand, you are still trying to figure out what your brand narrative should be, here's a simple exercise you can finish in a day that will help you find your way.

To help illustrate the exercise, let's go back to the MCU, *Game of Thrones*, and *Star Wars*. As we said before, these franchises succeeded because their creators started with the customer experience in mind and then built the brands that could best deliver it. Sure they are billion-dollar juggernauts now. But, in the beginning, before the first film or television episode, their creators were just like you, wondering what their brand story should be. And, like you can do now, they started by asking themselves six fundamental story building (and marketing) questions:

WHO are the characters people will care enough about to follow? (Who are we trying to reach with this brand?)

WHAT story are we going to tell? (What extensions will help us connect the brand with consumers?)

WHERE will these stories take place? (Where can we connect these stories to consumers?)

WHEN will the stories take place? (What should our timeline be for releasing each part of the story?)

HOW will the stories ultimately end? (How can we best connect these stories to the consumers who love them?)

WHY are these stories being told? (Why will they matter to consumers?)

Have you ever stopped and asked these six basic questions about your brand? Sometimes in marketing and advertising we get so caught up in the complex that we forget to slow down and ask the simple questions that offer clarity and direction. If you are building your brand, answer these six questions first. Answer them honestly and you will know who you are.

Consider for a second all the people who have touched the MCU, all the people who have worked on *Star Wars*, all the people involved with *Game of Thrones*. The collective genius in that group is staggering. And while they didn't all have this exact set of questions, they most likely started with similar queries.

Determining who you are and starting with the end in mind allows everyone involved in building the brand to share in both the vision and the mission. But even more, it's the only thing that allows your team to embrace creativity, innovation, and change and still arrive at the agreed upon destination.

◇◇◇◇◇◇

SO WHAT ABOUT THE CULTURE?

As we noted at the beginning of the chapter, building a transcendent culture is imperative for building a brand that lasts. Unless you're a one-man band (and what fun is that?), your brand and the brand experience you deliver to consumers is a collective reflection of everyone who works in your operation. If your culture embraces the requisite elements we talked about in Chapter 10 (safety, vulnerability, purpose, belonging, creativity, connection, and North Star Leadership), your brand will reflect that. On the other hand, if your culture is toxic and your people feel unsafe, threatened, aimless, alone, suffocated, ostracized, and without any meaningful leadership, then guess what? That's also what your brand and your customer experience will reflect.

No matter what it is you're selling, brand and culture go hand in hand. You can do the best job in the world at starting with the end in mind and understanding how you want to map out your brand, but if you're building that brand in an unhealthy environment with vitriolic leadership, if you ever do succeed, it will take twice as long and cost ten times as much.

In Chapter 12, you'll find checklists and blueprints to help you build a meaningful and lasting culture. Nothing is more important to the long-term success of your company. But don't just take our word for it. Listen to the business titans who have changed the world:

> *"Clients do not come first. Employees come first. If you take care of your employees, they will take care of the customers."*
> – Richard Branson, Virgin CEO

> *"Employees who believe management is concerned about them as a whole person—not just an employee—are more productive, more satisfied, more fulfilled. Satisfied employees mean satisfied customers, which leads to profitability."*
> – Anne M. Mulcahy, Xerox former CEO

> *"Culture eats strategy for breakfast, lunch, and dinner."*
> – Mark Fields, Ford Motor Company former President & CEO

> *"If you are lucky enough to be someone's employer, then you have a moral obligation to make sure people do look forward to coming to work in the morning."*
> – Howard Schultz, Starbucks CEO

"You can build a much more wonderful company on love than you can on fear."

– Kip Tindell, The Container Store Co-Founder

"The stronger the culture, the less corporate process a company needs. When the culture is strong, you can trust everyone to do the right thing. People can be independent and autonomous. They can be entrepreneurial."

– Brian Chesky, Airbnb CEO

<><><><><>

FOOTNOTES

[1] Box Office Mojo (www.boxofficemojo.com/), Franchises, Marvel Cinematic Universe (as of Oct. 1, 2019).

[2] Josef Adalian, "Nearly 20 Million People Have Already Watched The *Game Of Thrones* Finale," *Vulture.com*, May 20, 2019.

[3] *Game of Thrones*, IMDB.com

[4] "Box Office History for Star Wars Movies," The Numbers: Where Data and the Movie Business Meet, Oct. 1, 2019.

[5] Box Office Mojo, Franchises, Star Wars (as of Oct. 1, 2019) *Note: At the time of this writing, the final film in the Star Wars saga, Star Wars: The Rise of Skywalker, had not yet been released in theaters.*

12

⬦⬦⬦⬦⬦⬦

BUILDING AN EXTRAORDINARY CULTURE

7 Steps to Creating a Lasting Company and Brand

Just like building a company or a brand, building a lasting culture takes time and accountability. It takes vision and leadership. And as much as we wish it didn't, it takes patience and faith. That's not a contemporary problem. People have been dealing with patient growth, or a lack thereof, for fifteen hundred years. No doubt, you've heard, "A journey of a thousand miles begins with a single step." It's a Chinese proverb from the 6th Century.[1] "Rome wasn't built in a day,"[2] was written in 1538. And as contemporary leaders like U.S. Army General Creighton W. Abrams, Jr. and South African Bishop Desmond Tutu have reminded us, "When eating an elephant, take one bite at a time."[3][4]

One of the foundational tenets of the LOOMIS culture is that "where we go one, we go all." A huge part of living into that idea is communicating honestly about where we are as an agency and where we're going, not just among the management team, but to everyone in the company. It's not always easy to do that week by week, or even month by month. So twenty years ago, we started holding quarterly "Blueprint Meetings" where we looked at the good, the bad, and the ugly from the previous three months, finishing with a look at what the agency forecast looked like ahead. Each of our nearly eighty meetings has been held off campus at a local restaurant from 2pm until right about Happy Hour. It's a time for us to build each other up, but it's also a time for complete vulnerability and transparency. We talk about what we're doing strategically. We review creative much like Pixar does in their "braintrust" meetings. When things are going well, we celebrate together. When they're not, we talk honestly about that, too. And throughout the meeting, every member of the team knows they can ask any question and get a straight answer. Not every meeting is perfect. But the fact that we've pulled off the Blueprint every quarter for twenty years has forced us to pay attention. It's required us to talk about what's working and what isn't, and, collectively, it's helped us stay on course.

You can build an extraordinary culture in your own company even if reading this qualifies as your first step. Hear that again. You can build an extraordinary culture even if reading this sentence qualifies as your first step. It may seem like a Herculean task (because it is), but you can do it, and the good news is that you don't have to reinvent the wheel. To help you, we've included checklists throughout this chapter for the seven elements from Chapter 10 that make for a lasting culture. Think of it as your blueprint. That's not to say this is a "connect the dots" or a "paint by numbers" process. It's not. Every culture is unique and yours will be also. You may find there are some areas where you are already strong, and others where you need work. You may validate that your present culture is working well, or find that you're building from scratch. Wherever you are, the key to growth is moving forward. It's our hope that the following checklists will give you a great place to start building.

◇◇◇◇◇◇

BUILDING THE (CULTURAL) MAGNIFICENT SEVEN

SAFETY

Everyone wants to feel safe–physically, psychologically, emotionally, and spiritually. When most of us start our careers, we take that for granted. Why wouldn't a company provide a safe environment? Why wouldn't they allow me to ask questions and voice my opinion? Why wouldn't leadership provide a nurturing, supportive environment that's inclusive and encourages everyone's best work? The longer you've worked in this business (or any business), and the more companies you've worked for, the more you understand the answers to those questions aren't as simple as they should be. Safety at work is not a given. But it's absolutely required to build an exemplary culture.

Questions You Need to Ask Regarding Safety:
- Do our employees feel physically safe at work?
- Do our employees feel psychologically safe at work?
- Do our employees feel emotionally safe at work?
- Do our employees feel spiritually safe at work?

- Does our management team lead in a way that makes people feel safe?
- Do our employees feel safe voicing their opinions without repercussion?
- Do our employees feel safe respectfully challenging leadership without repercussion?
- Do we have a plan for what to do in the event of an unsafe situation? If so, have we discussed it with our employees?
- Have we established a protocol for what employees who don't feel safe should do?
- Do we hear our employees concerns about safety? Do I?

What You Need to Build Safety Into Your Culture:

- A willingness to hear concerns about safety and the resolve to make them right
- A survey that allows your team to offer their perspectives regarding all aspects of company safety
- A small, diverse project team of trusted, non-management team members who will review the survey findings and make recommendations on steps forward

THE BLUEPRINT

1. Hold an honest, robust conversation about safety with company leadership. Try to identify any clear concerns regarding physical, psychological, emotional, or spiritual safety at your company.

2. Commit to getting and listening to genuine feedback from your employees.

3. Choose a small, diverse group (5 – 9) of trusted, non-management employees to head up a special company project. As much as possible, the project team you choose should reflect diversity of gender, race, age, and religion. Interview members to ensure their commitment. If anyone is lukewarm or uncommitted about serving on the project team, find someone else who is eager to serve.

4. Hold a meeting with the small group to explain both the details of the project and how important it is to the company. Make sure the small group understands that you are empowering them to help build an extraordinary company culture and that you look forward to hearing their recommendations.

5. Explain to your entire team the company's new focus on building a great culture and that the first step is assessing company safety. Share with them the seven foundational tenets of exceptional culture and that you are committed to examining each one and making changes where necessary to move your company forward. If you can meet with the entire company, do it. If not (as in the case of offices in multiple cities or countries), cut a video where you deliver the same message, and email it to the company welcoming any feedback. Then, have the leaders of each office hold a discussion there. Do not just shoot off an email and expect people to engage.

6. Deploy the safety survey to your employees. Use your management team and influential team members to encourage 100% participation. Give people adequate time to complete the survey.

7. Aggregate the surveys. Have your project team review the findings and present a plan to you with recommendations for next steps forward. Reward the project team in some way for a job well done.

8. Discuss the recommendations with your management team, and make changes where necessary to bolster safety, starting with the easiest and most visible changes to show progress to your employees. Follow through on every concern.

9. Until every safety concern is addressed, give quarterly updates to your company about ways you have addressed safety concerns. Where possible, include pictures and progress reports about issues being addressed. All concerns should be addressed within 12 months.

∞∞∞∞

SIGNS OF SUCCESS

The sense of feeling safe is much like breathing, in that we don't always pay attention to it until something happens to threaten it. For some in your company, addressing safety concerns will be game changing. For others, they may barely notice. But make no mistake, creating an environment where people feel safe is imperative to your culture. When people feel safer, they also feel more confident. Conversations and brainstorms will be freer and more robust. People will be more open to sharing ideas both with each other and with management. Culturally, you will feel a greater sense of collective empowerment and renewed confidence as, together, your team looks for ways to support each other, deliver for your clients, build your company, and share in your success.

VULNERABILITY

Of all the qualities that make for a great leader, vulnerability has to be the hardest. Even if you buy into why being vulnerable is important and valuable to your company's big picture, letting down your guard, taking off your armor, and allowing yourself to be completely open with those you're leading still flies in the face of human nature. That's why for generations vulnerability has implied weakness, and who wants to be weak?

Thanks in large part to the work of Dr. Brené Brown, we are changing the way we look at vulnerability. We are starting to see that while, yes, stripping off a layer of protection can be seen as weakness, it can also be seen as the ultimate sign of authenticity and trust. It's not a switch you can just flip on. Opening yourself up takes time, introspection, and a lot of conversation with people you trust. But it's worth it. The question is, are you really willing to go there? And if not, why not? Because without some level of vulnerability, you can't build a great culture. Without vulnerability, there is only so far you can go as a leader.

Questions You Need to Ask Regarding Vulnerability:

- Do we as leaders and as an organization understand what it means to be vulnerable?
- Am I willing to be vulnerable and open with my team?
- Are the other members of the management team willing to be vulnerable with each other and the people they lead?
- Can we ask our team members to be vulnerable without taking advantage of that vulnerability?
- Where do we need to be more vulnerable in our leadership?
- What are we afraid of?

What You Need to Build Vulnerability Into Your Culture:

- A willingness to be more personally vulnerable with your team
- Information to share with your team about how to be more vulnerable and the advantages it brings
- A willingness and a plan to incorporate more vulnerability into the culture of your company
- Copies of *Daring Greatly* by Brené Brown and *The Culture Code* by Daniel Coyle to give to your employees

∞∞∞∞∞

THE BLUEPRINT

1. Schedule a leadership meeting to discuss the concept of vulnerability. Make it a serious but relaxing conversation over lunch, or in the afternoon with beverages. If you can have the

discussion offsite, even better. Listen to what your team has to say, and then share how you feel and why you believe adding vulnerability to the company is important.

2. Provide copies of *Daring Greatly* and *The Culture Code* to your leadership team.

3. Over the course of two to three months, hold a management "book club" during lunch where you discuss the concepts in *Daring Greatly* and *The Culture Code* and how you can incorporate them into your daily interactions within the company.

4. Quarterly, during your leadership meetings, make a point of discussing vulnerability and how well the team is or isn't incorporating vulnerability into the company culture.

5. When you feel like management is walking the walk, share what you've been studying with the rest of your company, encouraging them to read the books and apply the lessons to their own roles in the company.

∞∞∞∞∞

SIGNS OF SUCCESS

When you allow yourself to be vulnerable with your team and when you are honest enough to say, "I don't have all the answers," and, "I need you to help make this thing go," when culturally, "I don't know," and, "I need help," become acceptable answers, a powerful shift will start to happen. As you lower your guard, so will others. As you increase your empathy, so will others. As you begin leading from a place of we rather than me, you will find collective buy-in like you've never seen. The shift from "here's what *you* need to do" to "here's what *we* need to do" is subtle but powerful. And when your company becomes *their* company, your forward progress will be exponential.

PURPOSE

Of all the elements a transcendent culture comprises, purpose may be the most galvanizing. It's also the one we overthink the most. How many times have you and your management team gathered to discuss your company's purpose? Your direction? Who you want to be when you grow up? We bring in consultants, we go on retreats, and we grind to figure out who it is we're meant to be. It's a worthy quest, but sometimes it's easy to lose the forest for the trees. If the goal is to build a lasting, engaging, inspiring company that people want to spend their careers being a part of, what lies at the heart of that for you? What do want to be known for? What lighthouse beacon of an idea would you be proud to grow your company around? When you invest the time and energy to figure out your purpose, you give your team something noble to align with. And for maybe the first time ever, you will all begin to row in the exact same direction.

Questions You Need to Ask Regarding Purpose:
- What is our reason for being? Why does this company need to exist?

- Why is what we do important? Drill down by asking that question 5-10 times.
- Why is the world a better place because this company is in it?
- Do we presently have a collective purpose, and if so, are we all in agreement about what it is?
- What core values do our team members find meaningful? Are those core values reflected in this company?
- One hundred years from now, what would you like people to remember about this company?
- Is that something that excites, energizes, and inspires our team?

What You Need to Build Purpose Into Your Culture:

- The commitment as a leader and a management team to accept the invitation to search for your genuine purpose until you find it
- A survey that allows your team to offer their perspectives regarding core values they find meaningful and the degree to which those core values are reflected in your present organization
- A willingness to hear and address any incongruencies between the core values your employees find meaningful and the ones reflected in your company
- A commitment from your management team to invest the time and effort necessary to research, discuss, and define your purpose

THE BLUEPRINT

1. Share with the management team your intention to explore your company's purpose. Ask each team member by name for their personal commitment to the process.

2. Ask your team to write up a brief description of which core values are meaningful to them and why. Then have them make a list of the core values they believe are presently reflected in the company.

3. Distribute a quick core values survey to your company asking your team to weigh in on what values they find meaningful and what core values they see at work in the company.

4. Schedule a focused one-day off-site meeting (or if time and finances allow, a two-day off-site with a team dinner the night before). At the meeting, discuss the results of the core values exercise comparing personal and company values. Pay attention to how well the core values exercise matches up between management and the rest of your team.

5. If your company has a recognized purpose, discuss how well you are or aren't living into it. If you are finding your collective purpose through this exercise, discuss what you love about your company, what inspires and energizes both you and your employees, and what single idea you would be most proud to build your company around.

6. Once you settle on a collective purpose (this may take more time than a one- or two-day offsite), identify a small number of non-management team members you trust to have a confidential conversation. Share the purpose with them and genuinely listen to their feedback. You're not there to convince them it's right. You're there to listen to how it lands with them. Are they excited and inspired, or indifferent?

7. If the collective feedback is positive, move forward. If it's negative, explore the reasons why and consider that perhaps you haven't yet found your company's genuine purpose. If that's the case, revisit your management team discussion and consider adding 4-5 trusted non-management team members to your meeting with the management team and start again.

8. Once you have settled on your company purpose, look for ways to incorporate it into the company culture. Review it at the beginning of meetings. Have it printed and displayed in a prominent place in the company. Wherever possible, look for actionable opportunities that are congruent with the values your purpose is based on. For instance, let's say your purpose was the LOOMIS purpose: "To help challenger brands win—in a way that honors every stakeholder in the process." The next five questions you need to ask are:

- How do we live into that purpose in regard to our clients?
- How do we live into that purpose in regard to our employees?

- How do we live into that purpose in regard to our vendors and partners?
- How do we live into that purpose in regard to the consumer?
- How do we live into that purpose in regard to the communities where we work and live?

9. Answer those questions. Watch how they galvanize your people and your efforts, and then lean in hard and fulfill your purpose.

∞∞∞∞

SIGNS OF SUCCESS

Remember what Daniel Coyle said about purpose in *The Culture Code*. Coyle wrote, "Purpose isn't about tapping into some mystical internal drive, but rather about creating simple beacons that focus attention and engagement on the shared goal."[5] Purpose is *all* about rallying the troops around the authentic core values you believe in and can deliver. It's not a lot harder than that. When your team aligns around purpose and you begin to view your world through that prism, you will begin to see opportunities that you didn't see before. Pieces that seemed fractured will start to come together, and you will find that when you and your team are congruent to your core values, you will be better, more authentic, and effective leaders, and the people you work with at every level will notice.

BELONGING

We all have a deep down need to belong. Not a want. A need. It goes without saying why we need the love and connection that comes with belonging in our private lives. But we also need it when we walk into the office. And so does every person who has committed themselves to your company. There was a time in this country (when businesses were primarily run and dominated by men) when things like love, belonging, connection, intimacy, and vulnerability were seen as soft, emotional, and largely unfit for any kind of professional environment. Thankfully, that is changing. Ultra-competitive, cutthroat Thunderdomes are being replaced with cultures where things like inclusion, diversity, and emotional connection are not only encouraged, but required. Not because it's politically correct, but because it's smart business. When people feel a bond and a friendship with their co-workers, they stay. They work harder. They contribute more. Which prompts the question: When was the last time you did or said something to make your team feel like they belong?

Questions You Need to Ask Regarding Belonging:
- Do the people in our company feel a sense of belonging to our organization?
- Are *inclusive* and *diverse* words our employees would use to describe our culture? Would people outside the company describe us that way?
- What are we doing on a regular basis to foster a sense of belonging in our company?
- What, if anything, do we do for new employees to help them

feel like they belong to our community?

• Do we pay attention to whether or not our team feels a sense of belonging?

What You Need to Build Belonging Into Your Culture:

• A genuine understanding that belonging is foundational to any great culture

• A survey that gives your team members a chance to offer honest feedback about levels of belonging, diversity, and inclusion in your organization

• A willingness to hear and address any incongruencies between how you and your employees experience belonging, diversity, and inclusion in your company

• A commitment from your management team to invest the time and effort necessary to better understand how important belonging, diversity, and inclusion are to your organization and how to improve any shortcomings

◇◇◇◇◇◇

THE BLUEPRINT

1. Have an honest, vulnerable discussion with your management team about the state of belonging in your company. Do your leaders feel like they belong at the company? Do they feel a sense of belonging among each other? Do they perceive that the rest of your employees feel a sense of belonging to the company and among each other?

2. Ask your management team to make a list of things that would increase a sense of belonging in your company. In a meeting, review the lists and discuss how well you as a leadership team and a company could incorporate what's on the list into your culture.

3. Identify the top five things your team believes could improve the sense of belonging in your organization. Every month, focus on one of those things and look for ways to incorporate it into your culture. For instance, if "be friendlier" is on the list, you could establish a speaking tradition where employees are encouraged to say hello when they pass each other. You could set aside fifteen minutes a day to walk the halls and have positive conversations with your employees. You could smile more.

4. Quarterly, during your leadership meetings, make a point of discussing belonging and how well the team is (or isn't) taking steps to increase a sense of belonging into the company culture.

5. Hold a special meeting with your management team to discuss diversity in your company. Encourage complete honesty and transparency. Start by having everyone write down a diversity score for the company on a scale of one to ten, with ten being "completely diverse" and one being "no diversity at all." Then, have an honest discussion with your management team about their perspectives on diversity and inclusion in your company. Include HR in the meeting to offer another perspective. If you don't have an HR expert, arrange for one to sit in on the meeting

to help identify any blind spots. In your discussion, consider things like race, gender, age, sexual orientation, religion, disabilities, and even things like thinking style, personality, and life experience. At the end of the meeting, have your team write down a new diversity score for the company. Compare the two and discuss any changes.

6. After the diversity meeting, make a list of things you can do to increase diversity in your company and make a commitment to consider them as you hire.

7. Every quarter, revisit the topic of diversity and whether you are progressing toward being more inclusive.

SIGNS OF SUCCESS

Belonging isn't about fitting in or acclimating. It's about feeling like you are a valued part of something bigger than yourself. When cultures foster a healthy sense of belonging and embrace inclusion and diversity, the people in them no longer focus on what makes them different, instead harnessing the power of shared vision and what they can accomplish together. That's not to say there will never be differences of opinion. There will be, and that's a good thing. Diversity of ideas, perspectives, and solutions only makes you stronger. Don't be afraid to challenge stale, homogeneous thinking. Newer isn't always better. But many times, it is.

CREATIVITY

Every great culture embraces creativity or it dies. Of all the elements that make for transcendent culture, creativity is the most dynamic. No matter what kind of business you lead, your success and your survival depends on generating great ideas and their ability to move you forward. At any given moment, the power of a new idea can change momentum, chart a new course, or simply make what you're currently doing better. The largely untapped secret is that creativity can come from anywhere in your organization. Yes, you may have trained creative professionals who are better at the creative thing than others and we're not taking anything away from them. Siloing your creative production into a small group of people makes complete sense for a division of labor. But if that's the only place you're looking for creative ideas to solve problems, or spark inspiration, it's at best myopic and at worst dangerous.

Which would you rather have—more ideas to choose from, or fewer? Empowering every member of your team to contribute creatively does more than give them permission to create. It makes them feel safer, encourages them to be vulnerable, gives them purpose, and helps them feel connected to the rest of your company. Empowering creativity supports every other element that makes for great culture. And it allows you to ask the two most important questions in business: "What if?" and "Why not?"

Questions You Need to Ask Regarding Creativity:

• Are we adequately harnessing the power of creativity in our company?

- Have we siloed the creative process into too few people or departments?
- What would it look like to empower people in our company creatively?
- Do we have the creative leadership to manage a greater focus on creativity across the company?
- Are we committed to becoming a more creative organization?

What You Need to Build Creativity Into Your Culture:

- A commitment to the time and effort required to become a more creative organization
- An understanding from your "creative professionals" that this effort in no way minimizes their role, their work, or their expertise; this is about the organization getting stronger collectively
- A willingness and a plan to infuse creative exercises into your company culture
- Copies of *Creativity, Inc.* by Ed Catmull, *Thinkertoys* by Michael Michalko, and *The Imagineering Workout* by The Disney Imagineers to share with your employees

∞∞∞∞∞

THE BLUEPRINT

1. Schedule a leadership meeting to discuss your perspectives on creativity, where it's strong in your company, and where it can be improved. Make it a fun, engaging conversation with a creative

exercise to kick things off. Listen to what your team has to say, any concerns they may have, and, most importantly, to their ideas.

2. Provide copies of *Creativity, Inc.* and *Thinkertoys* for your leadership team.

3. Over the course of 2-3 months, hold a series of creative lunches where the management team discusses *Creativity, Inc.* and the Pixar approach to creativity. Discuss how you could incorporate some of the same approaches into your company.

4. Once a month as a management team, agree on a challenge facing the company, and have each team member come up with solutions using one or more exercises in *Thinkertoys*. Share your solutions and discuss which exercises worked best for creative problem solving.

5. Once the management team has gone through three creative exercises, have each team member talk with those they manage about the company's commitment to increasing creative thinking from everyone.

6. Each month, brief the company (or sections of the company if it's a large organization) on a challenge facing one of your clients or brands, and give everyone two weeks to come back with at least one idea for how to solve it. Give the ideas to the account and creative teams who handle that client or brand, and challenge them to incorporate the best ideas into their plans.

7. Once per quarter, as a company, choose one philanthropic challenge and ask the team to come up with creative solutions for how to solve it. Assign a budget to the solution. Set a deadline for submissions and then allow the company to vote for the best idea or ideas. For instance, in September, what impactful thing could we do to help the homeless with winter coming? You have a $2,500 budget. Go.

8. Provide copies of *Thinkertoys* and *The Imagineering Workout* for people to use for brainstorming creative challenges.

9. Challenge your "creative professionals"—your creative department and marketing team—to come up with at least one BIG traffic/sales-driving idea per quarter for one of your clients, brands, or your company. Have your creative department hold monthly meetings to review and discuss big ideas.

∞∞∞∞∞

SIGNS OF SUCCESS

There's a distinctive energy that comes with increasing creativity in your organization. It's an addictive, empowering energy that primes our competitive natures and drives us to solve seemingly unsolvable problems. Coming to work becomes fun. One burst of creative energy fuels the next. And your team members will look forward to working together to create, to compete, and to win. For challenger brands, creativity is your competitive advantage. Let the brand leaders outspend you all day long. As long as they aren't outthinking you, you're still in the game.

CONNECTION

As we mentioned before, connection is one of the most essential elements for holding your culture together. Where belonging feels more emotional, connection connotes a more tangible, physical bond that can only be measured in relationships. Real connection happens when the people inside your culture feel included, trusted, and invited to be a genuine part of something bigger than themselves. Connection is personal. And it's lasting. As easy as that sounds, it's not always. People are intricate. Feelings are complicated. Life and work are hard to balance. Fostering connection requires intention and constant cultivation from everyone in your organization. But when it's done well, it's the one tether that can hold you all together no matter what the world throws at you.

Questions You Need to Ask Regarding Connection:
- Do we, as the management team, feel genuinely connected to each other?
- Do our employees feel a strong sense of connection with company leadership?
- Do our employees feel a strong sense of connection with each other?
- Are there things in our company that are detrimental to building connection?
- What could we be doing to foster a greater sense of connection in our company?

- What actions do we take to address a situation where one of our people is feeling disconnected?

What You Need to Build Connection Into Your Culture:
- A genuine understanding of the role connection plays in building a culture that lasts
- A survey that gives your team members the chance to offer honest feedback regarding their level of connection to company leadership, their immediate manager, and each other
- A commitment to addressing any immediate lack of connection that surfaces from your team
- A long term commitment from your management team to invest the time and effort necessary to build stronger connection within your culture

THE BLUEPRINT

1. Meet with your leadership team offsite in a relaxed, private environment. Have each member answer the following questions about each other on a piece of paper. Allow one minute for each person in the room:

   a. Where did the person grow up?
   b. Where did the person go to college?
   c. What are the names of the person's spouse/significant other and children if they have any?

    d. Name two of the person's favorite foods.

    e. Name three things the person likes to do outside of the office.

When you're finished, compare answers. See how well you know even basic facts about each other. To avoid embarrassing anyone, have one person read the answers anonymously.

2. Discuss the concept of connection and the role you believe it plays in building a great culture. Have a genuine, honest, vulnerable conversation about the sense of connection you have with each other and where, if anywhere, it could be improved.

3. Have each manager meet with their teams and repeat the exercises in steps 1 and 2.

4. Concept a series of team building exercises and events that you can implement into your culture to help foster connection between team members and departments. These could include things like departmental outings, group lunches, celebrations, work anniversary acknowledgements, weekly company gatherings, pairing up veteran employees with new employees, book clubs, etc.

5. As key leaders, make a point of spending time with people in your company. Ask them how they are. Look them in the eye and really listen to what they say. Make sure they understand you genuinely care about them and value their contribution to the company.

6. Quarterly, during your leadership meetings, make a point of discussing connection and whether it feels as though people are more connected, or less. Take steps to build connection wherever and whenever possible.

7. Regularly do something thoughtful for the people in your organization who would least expect it.

∞∞∞∞

SIGNS OF SUCCESS

Genuine connection is a tough thing to measure. But you can feel it. And you'll definitely feel when it's absent from your culture. When your team feels connected, the office atmosphere will be more positive. People will be more agreeable. Disagreements will be resolved more quickly. And you'll feel a strong sense that everyone is pulling in the same direction. When people are truly connected, they don't just fight for themselves. They fight for each other. They fight for leadership and their clients. And they fight for everything they believe your company or your brand can be. That spirit of togetherness and connection is what built our country. *E pluribus unum*—"From many, one." That's the power of connection.

NORTH STAR LEADERSHIP

Of the seven essential elements for building a great culture—safety, vulnerability, purpose, belonging, creativity, connection, and North Star Leadership—this last one is all you. That's not to say you're the only leader, even if you are the leader at the top of your organization. What it means is that only you can do what it takes to become the person worthy of leading your team, your clients, and your organization. They don't need a manager. They need a beacon of clarity. They need an inspired thinker. They need a champion who can build them up and lead them into the battle for their professional existence. Are you willing to be that leader? Are you willing to invest the time and effort it takes to be an exceptional leader? It's a lifelong process. But thankfully, it's one you can start right now if you're just catching up.

Questions You Need to Ask Regarding Leadership:

- Where am I on my leadership journey? What are my strengths and weaknesses as a leader, and what am I doing to address them?
- Am I leaning into the other six essential elements for building a great culture?
  - Am I creating a safe environment for my team to work in?
  - Am I vulnerable with my leadership team and our other employees?
  - Do I live and lead with a purpose in mind both for myself and my company?
  - Do I foster a sense of belonging in our organization?
  - Do I encourage and embrace creative thinking from everyone in our company, believing great ideas can come from anywhere?
  - Do I feel a strong connection with my leadership team and the people in our company?

- Do I value constant learning and read on a regular basis to enhance and expand my leadership abilities?
- Do I live according to a strong set of core values?
- Am I taking a step forward toward being a better leader every day?

What You Need to Build North Star Leadership Into Your Culture:

- A learner vs. a knower mentality, realizing that the best leaders are constantly learning and never feel a compulsion to be the smartest person in the room
- A willingness and commitment to read and learn constantly
- A trusted circle of other leaders at your level who you can lean on for advice, mentorship, and confidential conversations
- A talented, trusted management team committed to helping you build a transcendent culture in your organization
- Smart, dedicated team members who are fully engaged in your company and leadership

⬦⬦⬦⬦⬦

THE BLUEPRINT

1. Take honest stock of where you are as a leader at this moment in time. List your strengths and weaknesses. What do you do really well? Where do you struggle? Make a list of your core values, your vision for where you want to be as a leader, and the purpose that will take you there.

2. Take an honest look at your company culture, keeping the seven essential building blocks in mind, and note which among the seven could be improved. Discuss with your management team, and create a plan of action for each element to start transforming your culture.

3. Think about where you want to take your company or your brand, what will inspire your team to get there, and what you need to do to get from where you are to where you want to be. Discuss it with your management team and, together, create a plan of action for transformation.

4. Start journaling daily. Spend five minutes at the beginning of the day and five minutes at the end of the day noting what went on that day, anything particularly good or challenging that happened, enlightening conversations you had, or positive steps that were taken in building the culture. Documenting your thoughts daily will give you a valuable record to review later.

5. Start reading regularly. There's no shortage of great books to read or listen to in addition to magazines, newspapers, blogs, and podcasts. The idea is to be constantly learning, listening to new ideas and taking bits and pieces of what works for others and incorporating them into what you're doing in your own leadership. Whether you know it or not, as a leader, your team and your clients expect you to stay current and know what's going on in the world. You don't need to be the smartest person in the room. But you do need to be informed. The list of our favorite

titles and authors at the end of this book is a great place to start. If you can't find time to read, get an audio book and listen.

6. Be more visible. As leaders, it's easy to hole up in our offices with the door shut to get things done. And while there's time for that, don't underestimate how meaningful it is for the people in your company to see you, to have a conversation with you, to spend real time with you. In positive cultures, you are who they look up to, and in many cases, aspire to be. Connect with them. Share your time with them, even if it means another thirty minutes on the back end of the day for you. Give them a reason to follow your leadership.

7. Understand that becoming a great leader and building a lasting culture don't happen overnight. They take time, planning, effort, and money. The key is to start and keep moving forward every day. You can do this. But that's the thing—you have to be the one to step up and make yourself into the leader you want to be. You don't have to do it alone. But everything begins with you.

∞∞∞∞∞∞

SIGNS OF SUCCESS

Exceptional leadership hinges as much on *how* we are, as *who* we are. That's why the most effective leaders view heading their companies and brands as a journey and not a destination. North Star Leadership is about understanding the privilege and responsibility you've been given. It's about working to develop the clarity of thought and the vision to inspire your team to do what no other company has done before. It's about building a culture that will not only attract the best talent, but keep them for years to come. Being an exceptional leader isn't easy. It takes extraordinary, sustained attention, focus, and effort. But when you can build a company with safety, vulnerability, purpose, belonging, creativity, connection, and leadership at its core, you will be in rarefied air where few ever fly.

◇◇◇◇◇◇

FOOTNOTES

[1] Lao Tzu. *Tao Te Ching*, Ch. 64.

[2] John Heywood, *A Dialogue Conteinyng the Nomber in Effect of all the Prouerbes in the Englishe Tongue* (c. 1538).

[3] "Creighton W. Abrams, Jr.," Wikiquote, Aug. 22, 2009.

[4] "There is only one way to eat an elephant, a bite at a time," Bishop Desmond Tutu, AZQuotes, Jan. 30, 2019.

[5] Daniel Coyle, *The Culture Code* (New York, NY: Bantam Books, 2018), 180.

13

WHEN GREAT CULTURES AREN'T GOOD

At LOOMIS, one of our evergreen cultural tenets is encouraging our people to be perpetual learners. To read, to watch, and to constantly experience other companies and brands soaking up great ideas wherever they find them. Like the greatest architectural marvels, it's one thing to design something extraordinary on paper, and quite another to actually build it. The same can be said of great company cultures.

Most of us will never have the pleasure of working in multiple extraordinary cultures. If we're fortunate, over the course of our careers, we might get to work in one or two. That's why, when it comes to building our own transcendent cultures, it's imperative we study those who have come before us and done things right. There's a reason companies who pay attention to culture thrive and endure. If we want to be one of them, the best thing we can do is pay attention and learn everything we can. Almost all great companies stand on the shoulders of the giants who came before them and that includes their company cultures.

Throughout this book, we've talked about a number of companies we think stand out from the rest and why we think so highly of them. No doubt you have your own favorites. Whether you're looking at our favorites or your own, dig in. See what works for you and what doesn't. Consider what these companies are doing to succeed, to build lasting cultures, and to draw and keep the best talent in the business. Make notes. Visit their websites. Experience their brands. Then consider which positive elements from these cultures you can use to transform your own culture. Just do it all knowing one thing—even the greatest cultures aren't for everyone. Almost all great companies stand on the shoulders of the giants who came before them and that includes their company cultures.

◇◇◇◇◇◇

GREAT CULTURE IS ALL ABOUT FIT

In Chapter 6, we discussed why HR and marketing need to share an office, and it's all in service of finding and hiring the people who will thrive in the culture you've created. Not every smart, personable, hard-working person is going to fit with your culture. That's not a bad thing. It's just reality. Some talent soars in a fast-paced, competitive, high-pressure environment. Others are destroyed by it. That doesn't make one person better than the other. It just means one is prime to work at a company like Amazon, while the other might be far more fulfilled working in a bookstore.

In 1992, best-selling author Gary Chapman wrote a monumental book called *The Five Love Languages* to help people in relationships better understand which actions are most meaningful to their partners. In the book, Chapman suggests that with our mates, each of us responds best to one of the following five "love languages:" Quality Time, Words of Affirmation, Receiving Gifts, Acts of Service, and Physical Touch.[1] One is not better than another. How you respond depends on who you are.

Take five wives or five husbands and consider the following five actions: watching a movie together, telling the other person how much they are loved and appreciated, bringing the person their favorite coffee and breakfast in bed, doing the dishes and cleaning up the kitchen without being asked, or giving the person a hug and a kiss. Each of us has one action that makes us feel more loved than another. Odds are, we respond to many of them. But each of us has our own primary love language, and Chapman contends that understanding your partner's love language and living into it is key to maintaining a happy, healthy, loving relationship.

There's a common belief that great employees will fit in and thrive in any great culture. But that's simply not true. Talented people respond to different cultural stimuli, just as people in relationships respond to different love languages.

In Jim Collins landmark book *Good to Great*, one of the great metaphors he uses is thinking of your company like a bus. As he elaborates on his website:

> *Those who build great organizations make sure they have the right people on the bus and the right people in the key seats before they figure out where to drive the bus. They*

always think first about who and then about what. When facing chaos and uncertainty, and you cannot possibly predict what's coming around the corner, your best "strategy" is to have a busload of people who can adapt to and perform brilliantly no matter what comes next. Great vision without great people is irrelevant.[2]

Great culture is all about fit. Building that culture starts with finding the people who should be on your bus.

Do a search of the best company cultures and you will find a thousand reasons why people think certain cultures are great, including many that don't exactly lean into the seven factors we laid out earlier for building a great culture. Some of them may even seem to run counter to those ideas. That doesn't make us right and them wrong, or vice versa. There are many ways to build a culture that works, and, as we've noted, not every culture fits every employee. Like a perfectly mixed song, every company reflects some aspect of safety, vulnerability, purpose, connection, creativity, belonging, and leadership. As a leader, your job is to mix a little more of this with a little less of that until your culture sounds perfectly balanced—to you. Set your levels. Play your music. Then, work like hell to find people who love the sound of your tune.

◇◇◇◇◇◇

DON'T STOP UNTIL YOU FIND THE CULTURE THAT'S RIGHT FOR YOU

For the majority of this book, we've been talking to company leaders about the importance of culture and how to build one. But we'd be remiss if we didn't also say a word to those of you not yet at the top who are trying to *find* a great culture.

As you probably know, finding a job at a company with an outstanding culture isn't the world's easiest task. For starters, culture isn't something that's talked about a whole lot, especially outside of the category leaders you read about in the press. We hear a lot about earnings, product offerings, promotions, and marketing. But of more than 5.6 million employers in the U.S.[3], only a small percentage truly stand out culturally. That's not because there's a scarcity of great cultures. There are thousands. You just don't hear about them.

Clearly, the bigger and more public a company is, the more you can find out about them and their culture. But keep in mind, big companies represent a very small percentage of companies. According to the 2016 Census Bureau's Annual Survey of Entrepreneurs, only 1.8% of American companies employ more than one hundred people.[4] That means of the 5.6 million U.S. companies, roughly one hundred thousand employ more than one hundred people. For all the Wall Street glory of the Fortune 500, this country is built on small and midsize businesses, and their cultures are just as crucial as the big boys. With one hundred employees or less, their cultures may even be more important.

So how do you find the culture that's best for you? And once you identify a company with a great culture, how do you give yourself the best chance to get a job there? Resume and experience clearly matter. But there's a lot more to it than just that. Whether you're looking for a company that's fast-paced or laid-back, big or small, major metro, or small town, here are twelve steps that should help you identify the kind of culture that's best for you and give you a much better chance of landing a job once you find it.

FIRST, UNDERSTAND YOUR ABSOLUTES

As the Greeks loved to say, "First, know thyself." Before you can start trying to find a culture where you can thrive, you need to understand who you are, what makes you tick, and in what environments you can do your best work. What, for you, is an absolute *yes* and what's an absolute *no*? Do you like a quiet workspace or to be in the middle of the action? Are interaction and collaboration a must, or are you happier working by yourself? Do you like a lot of direction or a little? Small cube or open concept? Travel or no travel? Dogs or no dogs? Strict rules or laid back and trusting? Sit down and make a very honest list of what it is you want in a company culture. You're not being a prima donna. This is your career, all forty years of it, and as long as you don't roll in demanding endless bowls of orange M&M's and a massage every Tuesday, you'll find the right fit.

DO YOUR RESEARCH

There's never been a better time in history to do research. Online search tools let you find all kinds of information both good and bad, about companies you're interested in, but keep in mind, from "unbiased" articles to reviews on websites like Glassdoor, much of the information out there is nothing more than one person's opinion. That's not to say those opinions aren't informed and 100% correct. Just don't read one or two articles, or reviews and decide whether a company is right for you or not. Start with a company's website. See what, if anything, they say about their culture, and then see if the other information you read matches what the company says. A couple of discrepancies could be easily explained away. A bunch, and there may be a bigger problem.

SEARCH "COMPANIES THAT _____."

When you're doing an online search for companies with the kind of culture you want, be explicit. If you want companies that allow dogs in the workplace, literally search for "companies that allow dogs in the workplace" (7.75 million results), and keep adding to your query to narrow down the results. Make a list of the ten things you most want from your workplace. Search for companies that fit your criteria and make lots of notes. Keep searching until you find companies that start overlapping on your different lists. No place is going to check every box, but you can get close.

LOOK FOR BOOKS WRITTEN ON THE COMPANY CULTURE

Clearly this works best for bigger, Fortune 500-type companies, but, no matter which company you're researching, search Google, Amazon, or Barnes & Noble to see what books have been written about the companies you're interested in. Even if they aren't explicitly about culture, many corporate books often mention or devote a chapter to culture. If you don't find any books about a specific company, keep checking back. Every year, more and more books are being written as companies realize culture is a very big deal.

REACH OUT TO PEOPLE YOU KNOW

As you're searching companies, go on LinkedIn and search your contacts to see if you know anyone who might have worked at the companies you're interested in. If not directly, they may be connected to someone who could help you. Quick conversations with people who have worked at a company you're exploring is an invaluable opportunity to hear a first-person account of what the company is really like. Again, it's a single person's opinion, but if it's someone you trust, pay attention. (Oh, and if you're not on LinkedIn, get on LinkedIn.)

WATCH HOW COMPANIES RESPOND TO CRISES

Corporate integrity isn't one of our essential cultural tenets, but only because it's such an obvious component of success, its inclusion goes without saying. How companies react when bad things happen can tell you a lot about who they really are.

In 1982, back before safety packaging was the norm, a psychopath in Chicago laced a number of bottles of Tylenol with potassium cyanide resulting in the deaths of seven people. Johnson & Johnson, Tylenol's parent company, could have handled the crisis a number of ways, from dealing with it locally to quietly ignoring it. They chose the safest and most expensive route, immediately pulling Tylenol from shelves nationwide (thirty-one million bottles with a value of more than $100 million) and quickly engineering safety packaging for their products. At the time of the deaths, critics predicted it could be the end of Tylenol as a brand. Less than a year after J&J's response, now broadly recognized as the blueprint for how to handle a corporate crisis, Tylenol had regained the highest market share of any over-the-counter analgesic in the U.S.[5]

In 2018, two African-American men were handcuffed and arrested in a Philadelphia Starbucks after a barista called police with a complaint the men were sitting in the shop without ordering anything. It turns out, the men were simply waiting for a friend to arrive. Again, there were any number of ways the coffee giant could have dealt with what was clearly an injustice. Within days, Starbucks CEO Kevin Johnson flew to Philadelphia to personally meet with the two men and offer a face-to-face apology. A month later, Starbucks shut down 8,000 stores nationwide for a day of racial-bias education.

These are just a few notable examples of how companies have dealt well with moments of crisis. If you want to know if a company is somewhere you'd be proud to work, look for how the leadership responds to situations that hold their cultures accountable. If a company stands strong and congruent with its principles and culture when things are at their lowest, it will surely sustain you when times are good.

LOOK AT "BEST PLACES TO WORK" LISTS

Search "best places to work" and you're likely to get about four billion results. Clearly, some are more helpful than others and you can always narrow them down. The point is, there's a lot of information online to help you find a great place to work that matches your list of cultural gotta haves. Lots of magazines now put out annual "Best Places" lists, as do most big city newspapers and chambers of commerce. Even smaller towns are starting to put out their own "favorites" lists that often include companies. Do your research, make your notes, and utilize "Best Of" lists to help you decide which companies are the best fit for you.

DON'T BE AFRAID TO ASK QUESTIONS

Your next step in the process is to get an interview at companies where you think you'd like to work. Hopefully, you've talked to contacts who have either worked there or know people who have, and you've gotten some good insights about what the company is really like. Interviews are the perfect place to ask questions. Companies with great cultures are proud of them and eager to fill positions with people who not only fit in with their culture, but who will add to it. Ask the people you interview with to tell you about their culture. Ask them what they love about working there. The more people you ask, the better picture you'll get.

TRY TO GET AN INTERNSHIP, OR SHADOW A DEPARTMENT WHERE YOU WANT TO WORK

While interviews last a few hours, internships can last for months. If there's no job available, but you really want to work somewhere, ask about an internship. If you can swing it financially, offer to take one that's unpaid. Even arranging to shadow someone for a day or a week in a department where you think you'd like to work can show you what a company's culture looks like up close.

Both allow you to observe the company quietly over time, and it gives you time to ask additional questions to people you could end up working with. As you gather information, keep one thing in mind—it's a snapshot. Even great cultures ebb and flow over time, and it's possible you could catch someone on a bad day. Unless it's something egregious, be careful not to make any decisions based on a single piece of evidence.

ASK TO SPEAK WITH PEOPLE WHO WORK AT THE COMPANY

If it's not possible to get an internship or to shadow someone, ask your interviewer if there are people in the company you could talk to or contact at a later time to ask additional questions about the culture. You don't want to be a pest, but as long as you're polite and show genuine interest, most companies should be happy to indulge your curiosity. This is especially true if you're coming right out of college, have done your homework, and show a genuine attraction to the culture the company is building.

LEAN INTO THE CULTURE

Congratulations! You landed a job at a company with a fantastic culture. Your job now is to lean into it fully and become one of the sustaining elements that not only maintains the culture, but makes it better. Look for places where you can affect positive change. Look for opportunities to participate, to lead, and when you are a healthy part of the culture, to innovate and make it even better. A company's culture is like a coral reef. There are hundreds of life forms living in a symbiotic relationship that's constantly evolving and every person in that environment has an obligation to leave it better than they found it.

HELP FIND THE NEXT YOU

The last puzzle piece to finding and maintaining a lasting culture is helping find the next generation of people who will love it and care for it as much as you do. If you are fortunate enough to have found an exciting, nurturing, fulfilling culture where you can build a career, part of your legacy should be making sure it lasts long enough for others to benefit. As we've noted repeatedly, finding companies with incredible cultures is rare. That makes them very special and something to be valued. Make discerning choices in adding to the ecosystem, but always make room for those who are different. They don't have to look like you, sound like you, or even be like you. All they have to do is be culturally committed. That's the secret that makes us all stronger.

◇◇◇◇◇◇

FOOTNOTES

[1] Gary Chapman, *The Five Love Languages: How to Express Heartfelt Commitment to Your Mate* (Chicago, IL: Northfield Publishing, 1992).

[2] Jim Collins, "First Who, Then What," Jim Collins' website, Jan. 30, 2020.

[3] "Facts & Data on Small Business and Entrepreneurship," SBE Council, Jan. 30, 2020.

[4] Ibid.

[5] "Chicago Tylenol Murders," Wikipedia, Jan. 14, 2020.

14

HOW CHALLENGERS REALLY WIN BIG

Who Needs Advertising?

Finally, a bit of treason as it relates to our own profession. Between the two authors of this book, we've stacked up more than sixty years of experience working in advertising agencies on hundreds of brands across virtually every consumer category, on campaigns both large and small. We love our profession and, more importantly, we've seen with our own eyes how the power of great advertising drives brand success.

Advertising offers creativity in service of capitalism, and we're proud of the work we've done to help crank the wheel of the free enterprise system and improve business performance for our clients. As students of the craft, we've long studied and admired the greats from early advertising legends like David Ogilvy, Leo Burnett, Mary Wells, and Bill Bernbach, to their modern-day offspring who've created brilliant campaigns and built some of the world's most powerful brands.

By now, you know challenger brands are what capture the

large parts of our imaginations and enthusiasm. But even within challenger brands, there's a special subset of brands we admire most of all. Ironically, it's those extraordinary challenger brands whose magnetic force is so strong, they draw consumers without the benefit of advertising campaigns and big media buys. According to 2018 estimates, there are more than thirteen thousand advertising agencies in the United States generating more than $45 billion in annual revenue,[1] but you won't find these unique challenger brands on any of their client rosters. These unusual brands rely on very little advertising—*if any at all*—for driving business performance. What's more, not only do many of these exceptional brands perform just as well as competitors that spend heavily on advertising, a number of them dramatically outperform their larger category rivals. Famous challenger brands like In-N-Out Burger, Trader Joe's, and REI spend next to nothing on advertising, yet they still manage to build and sustain enviable growth trajectories year in and year out.

In the notoriously competitive fast food category, a brand the size of In-N-Out Burger would typically spend in the neighborhood of $25 million annually on corporate advertising. Franchisees would also kick in an additional 2-3 percent on advertising to support their local market needs. The total ad budget for a restaurant chain kicking out $600 million in annual revenue like In-N-Out could easily top $40 million. But not the quirky burger maker from California. According to Kantar Media, in 2019, the entire company spent a little more than $2 million on advertising. Meanwhile, annual sales for an average In-N-Out Burger restaurant are a staggering $4.5 million. That's almost double the annual sales of a typical

McDonald's. (According to QSR, an average McDonald's makes $2.7 million).[2] By comparison to In-N-Out's $2 million, according to Kantar, category killer McDonald's lays out more than $650 million each year promoting the Golden Arches.

Look at Trader Joe's, another advertising anomaly. The company operates more than five hundred grocery stores with yearly sales north of $13 billion, but they spent less than $4,000 on advertising in 2018. You read that right. Less than $4,000. Most of us probably spend more on our company holiday parties than Trader Joe's lays out on advertising each year.

To be fair, that $4,000 is a measured media number reported by Kantar, which typically underreports actual spending on a company's total advertising. But still, Trader Joe's is not an advertising account you'll find a smart ad agency chasing around. A Vox report put it this way: "Trader Joe's does not participate in traditional advertising, never has sales, and is known for frustrating product shortages. Despite all this, it's one of the most beloved brands in the U.S."[3] Proving this very point, in 2019, Trader Joe's ranked first among the fifty-six largest grocery chains on dunnhumby's Retail Performance Index (RPI), which is based on a combination of strong positive consumer sentiment and financial performance.[4]

And how about specialty sporting goods retailer, REI? With 158 locations and $2.4 billion in revenue, this challenger brand competes in a category that includes Walmart, Dick's Sporting Goods, Academy, Bass Pro Shops, and Target. But unlike every other retailer in the space, REI succeeds without the benefit of significant spending on advertising. In 2019, the company posted its fifteenth straight year of record sales.[5] Not only did REI accomplish this without a big ad budget, it did so by using unconventional tactics that serve as the hallmark of challenger brands.

In 2015, REI started the #OptOutside tradition of closing all its stores on Black Friday to encourage their customers and employees to get outside rather than go shopping. It was a bold move considering retailers racked up more than $7 billion in consumer sales on Black Friday in 2019 alone.[6] No matter, just twenty-four hours into their very first #OptOutside initiative in 2015, REI's tradeoff was rewarded with more than 2.7 billion unpaid media impressions for the brand.[7] Not surprisingly, in the years since, the company's social media efforts, which are curated by employee brand evangelists, have become a primary driver for the brand.

While big brands grab the lion's share of headlines, scores of much smaller challenger brands like First United Bank, Milwaukee Electric Tool, Highland Homes, and many more like them across virtually every category, also drive great success with comparably low reliance on advertising.

With relatively little focus on paid media, First United Bank, based in tiny Durant, Oklahoma, has grown assets 10-20 percent in each of the last ten years to more than $10 billion. Since 2011, sales for Milwaukee Electric Tool have grown nearly 400 percent, dramatically outpacing category behemoths like Stanley Black & Decker, Makita, and HILTI. Highland Homes builds more than three thousand single-family homes exclusively in Texas year in and year out, a volume that makes them one of the leading homebuilders in the entire United States.

And over the past nine years, Highland has won eight consecutive People's Choice Builder of the Year awards, earning the kind of distinction that puts them in a brand category of their own, ahead of competitors who push their brands with aggressive ad campaigns. And yet, they've done very little advertising to date.

◇◇◇◇◇◇

BEST OF THE BRANDS

So, what exactly is going on here? Clearly, most brands are in no position to shut off their advertising programs and expect results anything like these. We'd hardly advise it. In fact, spending on advertising in the U.S. is on pace to climb to $260 billion by 2022. That's an increase in annual spending of nearly 60 percent from 2015.[8] Our Mad Men peers can breathe a collective sigh of relief because, while the landscape is always changing, the ad world is safe from any signs of imminent demise. That said, this fact only makes the performance of outlier challenger brands that buck the trend in spending even more impressive and all the more curious.

To be fair, it's not as if they're paying no attention at all to advertising and marketing. In fact, most of these brands have talented and very creative internal marketing teams focused on making the most of their limited resources. It's the comparably limited scale of their advertising efforts that's notable, not the complete absence of them. In fact, like REI, many of them make excellent use of less expensive social channels to help deepen customer connections and build meaningful brand engagement. Even so, these companies don't lead with advertising and marketing. They start with something that hopefully by now, you know is far more important for building an extraordinary brand.

Whether a company spends $4,000 or $40 million on their advertising, the challenger brands we admire most create unique marketplace distinction and drive business success by thinking culture first.

∞∞∞∞∞

WHAT WORKS FOR ONE, DOESN'T ALWAYS WORK FOR ALL

We've looked at how companies like Red Bull, Chick-fil-A, KTM, and others built their brands from the inside out by ensuring their brand values and cultural values were tightly aligned. They understand that when a company's brand and culture are operating in sync, the resulting synergy becomes highly attractive to customers. We refer to these brands as congruent because it's this tight alignment between brand and culture that allows them to carve out unique, distinctive positioning in their markets. More importantly, it helps them deliver on their most important consumer promises while holding myriad competitors at bay.

In truth, the vast majority of successful challenger brands rely on competitive levels of advertising spending to make their marketing work. Even well-aligned and high-performing brands need the pressure of consistent advertising and marketing campaigns to capture and hold the attention of customers. Challenger brands that do manage to thrive without the heavy winds of advertising at their backs do so by also maintaining sharp focus on one particular aspect of company culture that can have the effect of supercharging brand performance. Leaders at these companies are committed to being best-in-category employers.

We've talked about why leaders like The Container Store founder Kip Tindell take an active stand against the old "customers first" mantra that's so widely embraced by management and marketing pundits. The result? The kind of brand power that often transcends the need to rely on traditionally conceived advertising and marketing efforts. It's not a complete explanation, of course, and it's not intended to be. Companies that succeed without advertising do a lot of things right. But a zealously committed employee base can serve as a powerful activating agent for a brand. It often seems to explain the curious energy that animates the unusual brand performance of those that win without playing by the traditional rules of advertising and marketing.

A look through various "Best Places to Work" lists reveals a number of brands that either don't rely on much advertising at all, or are able to promote their brands in unique ways that bolster their already strong consumer preference. Not surprisingly, you'll find In-N-Out, Trader Joe's, and REI all over lists of the country's best employers. You'll also find brands like Chick-fil-A and Southwest Airlines on these lists, and while they do spend heavily on advertising, there's a big difference why they're there, and it's an important one.

While Chick-fil-A does invest in advertising, it doesn't choose to play the heavy promotional messaging and discount game like virtually every other fast food chain. Fast food advertising is frenetic. Advertisers hammer consumers from every angle with limited time offers and a never-ending barrage of new products to win their fleeting attention. Not Chick-fil-A. Their brand is so beloved, the company doesn't have to follow suit and try to discount its way to success. Instead, Chick-fil-A has been able to concentrate on messaging that further endears the brand to customers.

Running for more than two decades, the brand's famous "Eat Mor Chikin" campaign was only possible because the legendary commitment of its own employees allowed it to meet and exceed customer expectations consistently. The same is true for Southwest Airlines. While the airline category is notorious for banal ad campaigns selling destinations and a tiresome list of features and benefits, Southwest shows up very differently. It's a brand that's radically focused on customers, which has long been the singular unifying message of all the company's advertising. Southwest's advertising feels authentic because customers know the brand delivers on its promise. Again, that's because they've built their brand promises around the exceptional performance of employees who genuinely love what they do and who they do it for. Extremely high employee satisfaction is often a cultural feature among these extraordinary challenger brands, and it can serve as an activating agent for boosting brand strength. By creating energized work environments and focusing on employee engagement and satisfaction, these companies provoke high brand performance. When a brand's congruence is already high, the net effect can be to reduce the need to advertise the way other brands do. If your brand is what people think it's like to do business with you, your culture is what people think it's like to work with you.

◇◇◇◇◇◇

CHALLENGERS WIN WITH CULTURE

"We really view culture as our number one priority. We decided that if we get the culture right, most of the other stuff will just take care of itself."

— Tony Hsieh, CEO of Zappos

Back in 2015, a group of marketing thought leaders gathered at the annual Kellogg Marketing Leadership Summit to talk about the impact of company culture on business performance. Among those gathered, nearly all of them agreed that a company's culture had a direct and undeniable impact on the buying decisions of its customers. They agreed that the way customers feel about doing business with a company is inextricably linked to its culture. Yet, just over half of them felt as though their own company's culture supported their brand. Even worse, 20 percent said their company cultures were actively undermining their brands.[9]

Most of the summit attendees were marketers whose resumes included lists of industry leading blue chip brands like Coca-Cola, Kraft Foods, Merck, Cisco, and McDonald's. We certainly respect those brands, but frankly, we're not much interested in them. And it doesn't surprise us at all that companies of that size may struggle with the idea of aligning their cultures with their brands. It's the rare category leader that makes an appearance on a Best Places list. And as is so often the case, the very advantages of category leadership (like size and scale) can often become unwieldy barriers.

This is where the advantage goes to the challenger. But only if they make the choice to step up and make it so. It's easy to wag our fingers at the behemoths and cast aspersions about them claiming culture is important, but not following through. But how many of us are guilty of the very same thing? We get it. The idea of building and curating a great culture is overwhelming. It's bigger than any individual leader. Often, bigger than any one generation of leadership. And yet, like so many other challenges, the hardest part is taking the first step. The best time to plant a tree was twenty years ago. The next best time is today. What's stopping you from building the culture you want? It's clearly important to you, or you wouldn't have taken the time to read this book.

You have it in you to create a game-changing culture. All you have to do is take the first step. And forget the hard stuff. Start with imagination. Picture the kind of culture you want for your company. For your people. For yourself. Share the dream with those you trust. Lean into the camaraderie, the respect and the love you share for each other, and the brand you're committed to building. Look closely at the roles safety, vulnerability, purpose, belonging, creativity, connection, and focused leadership play in your company now, and how much better they could be. Take one step forward and live into the change you want to see.

Do that and one day, you'll wake up and realize your culture has helped make your brand a ten- or twenty-year overnight sensation. But even more, you'll also have the epiphany that building a transcendent culture wasn't really about a destination.

It was about taking the journey with the people you care about, all along.

∞∞∞∞

FOOTNOTES

[1] A. Guttman, "Advertising agencies in the U.S.—Statistics & Facts," *Statista*, Sept. 20, 2018.

[2] Chloe Sorvino, "Exclusive: In-N-Out Billionaire Lynsi Snyder Opens Up About Her Troubled Past and The Burger Chain's Future," *Forbes*, Oct. 10, 2018.

[3] Rebecca Jennings, "People Love Trader Joe's so much there are now professional Trader Joe's influencers," *Vox*, Nov. 6, 2019.

[4] Russell Redman, "Trader Joe's takes top spot on grocery retailer ranking," Jan. 10, 2019.

[5] Sean McCoy, "REI Posts Record Revenues for 15th Straight Year," *Gear Junkie*, April 9, 2019.

[6] Kelsey Lindsey, "5 takeaways from this year's Black Friday," *Retail Dive*, Nov. 30, 2015.

[7] Jeff Beer, "How REI is keeping the #OptOutside magic alive on Black Friday," *Fast Company*, Nov. 22, 2018.

[8] A. Guttman, "Media advertising spending in the United States from 2015 to 2022," *Statista*, Mar. 28, 2019.

[9] Dick Patton and A. Rory Finlay, "The Intersection of Brand and Culture," *EgonZehnder*, Nov. 15, 2016.

ACKNOWLEDGEMENTS

◇◇◇◇◇◇

As much as writing a book is a solitary activity, it cannot happen—and in our cases, wouldn't have happened—without the incredible support of our friends and families.

First, our eternal thanks to our wives and children, Melinda, Regan, and Jack Sullivan; and Ginger, Matt, and Caroline Tuggle. When it comes to our wives, both our fathers were quick to point out that we outkicked our coverage, and they were right. For nearly thirty years, Melinda and Ginger have been our unwavering support behind the scenes, our biggest cheerleaders out front, and our constant comfort and reassurance when agency-building was harder than we ever thought it would be. Between us, we are also beyond blessed to have four smart, passionate kids whose hearts are even bigger than their dreams. You all make us proud every day and we can't wait to see all the ways you make the world a better place.

To our LOOMIS family, this book would never have happened without you. When we set out to build the Agency in 1999, we agreed to take everything we loved about the places we'd worked before and use those things as the building blocks for a new agency. That was the beginning of the culture we have today, and you've all played a huge part in adding to it, curating it, and making it extraordinary. This book is as much yours as it is ours.

To Paul Loomis, Julie Ondrusek, Tina Tackett, Aimee Herron, Laura Cottongim, and Tre Nagella, thank you for two decades of leadership and friendship. We have both learned valuable, enduring lessons from being in relationship with each of you, and those lessons are reflected throughout this book. As we note at the end of the last chapter, building a great agency really isn't about the destination. It's about the journey and taking it with people you love and care for. It's been a blessing to take this ride with you.

Special thanks to all the people who helped us put this book together. Thanks to Tina Tackett for her endless encouragement and beautiful book design. Thanks to Kim Smith for proofreading, for her extensive publishing knowledge, and for her patience when we looked like deer in the headlights. Big thanks to our editor Jennifer Bussey for her many insights and for nursing us through our excessive comma issues.

A huge thank you to the mentors we've been fortunate enough to learn from and the hundreds of clients we've been proud to serve over thirty years in this business. We love what we do, and it has been a sincere privilege to work on your behalf.

Finally, because this is probably as close as either us will get to the Oscars®, the Emmys®, the Grammy Awards®, the Tonys®, or The Nobel Prize, to our Moms, and to our Dads who both passed on way too soon, we love you and we hope this makes you proud.

ESSENTIAL READING

The following is a list of our favorite books and the ones that have influenced our thinking and leadership the most over the past twenty years. Undoubtedly, there are other fantastic reads that aren't on this list. But if you start here and read even a fraction of these, you'll be way ahead of most business leaders and primed to become a high-performing challenger brand yourself.

CHALLENGER BRANDING, CULTURE, AND LEADERSHIP

Eating the Big Fish: How Challenger Brands Can Compete Against Brand Leaders – Adam Morgan

Start With Why – Simon Sinek

The Culture Code – Daniel Coyle

Daring Greatly and *Dare To Lead* – Brené Brown

Contagious – Jonah Berger

David and Goliath – Malcolm Gladwell

Becoming A Category Of One – Joe Calloway

Emotional Intelligence – Daniel Goleman

The Traveler's Gift – Andy Andrews

The Power of TED: The Empowerment Dynamic – David Emerald

Conscious Capitalism – John Mackey and Raj Sisodia

What Got You Here Won't Get You There – Marshall Goldsmith

Didn't See It Coming: Overcoming the 7 Greatest Challenges That No One Expects and Everyone Experiences – Carey Nieuwhof

BUILDING COMPANY CULTURES

Creativity Inc. (Pixar) – Ed Catmull

Powerful: Building A Culture of Freedom and Responsibility (Netflix) – Patty McCord

Covert Cows and Chick-fil-A: How Faith, Cows and Chicken Built An Iconic Brand (Chick-fil-A) – Steve Robinson

Nuts!: Southwest Airlines' Crazy Recipe For Business and Personal Success (Southwest Airlines) – Kevin & Jackie Freiberg

Ben & Jerry's Double Dip: How To Run A Values-Based Business and Make Money, Too (Ben & Jerry's) – Ben Cohen & Jerry Greenfield

Delivering Happiness: A Path To Profits, Passion and Purpose (Zappos) – Tony Hsieh

MARKETING AND ADVERTISING

The 22 Immutable Laws Of Marketing – Al Ries and Jack Trout

Influence and *Pre-Suasion: A Revolutionary Way to Influence and Persuade* – Robert Cialdini

Good To Great – Jim Collins

Fascinate and *How The World Sees You* – Sally Hogshead

Thinking Fast and Slow – Daniel Kahneman

Tribes – Seth Godin

The 5 Dysfunctions Of A Team – Patrick Lencioni

Thinkertoys – Michael Michalko

INDEX